PANORAMA OF WORLD ART

———————

ART OF NINETEENTH-CENTURY EUROPE

ART OF NINETEENTH-CENTURY EUROPE

Text by JÜRGEN SCHULTZE

HARRY N. ABRAMS, INC. Publishers NEW YORK

Front end papers:

CLAUDE-NICOLAS LEDOUX (1736–1806). *Design for House of the Director of the Loue River;*
part of project for the saltworks of Chaux, Arc-et-Senans (Franche-Comté). c. 1775.
Bibliothèque Nationale, Paris

Back end papers:

LEDOUX. *Design for House of the Rural Guards of Maupertuis.* c. 1779.
Bibliothèque Nationale, Paris

Translated from the German by Barbara Forryan

Standard Book Number: 8109-8017-7
Library of Congress Catalogue Card Number: 79-92913

Copyright 1970 in Germany by
HOLLE VERLAG GMBH, BADEN-BADEN
All rights reserved. No part of this book may
be reproduced without the written permission of the publishers
HARRY N. ABRAMS, INCORPORATED, NEW YORK
Printed in West Germany. Bound in the Netherlands

Contents

Introduction   (page 6)

Painting   (page 13)

Sculpture   (page 166)

Architecture   (page 202)

Bibliography   (page 253)

Chronological Tables   (page 256)

Index   (page 262)

Photo Credits   (page 264)

Introduction

It is customary to speak of "Baroque" and "Rococo" and to attempt to comprehend and differentiate between historical periods of art by means of terms such as "Gothic" or "Renaissance." The art of the nineteenth century, on the other hand, is generally considered within its chronological limits.

It is clear, however, that the strict chronological definition of the century is little more than a purely convenient arrangement. In order to provide a meaningful unity, almost all historical books and documents take a stage in the eighteenth century as their starting point. Even here, the dividing line is uncertain and is situated at many different times, but generally in connection with the French Revolution of 1789. At its outbreak, this was directed against the power of the nobles under the *ancien régime,* and against the Baroque nature of contemporary social structure with its religious basis—although it was from these very factors that the Revolution derived its vigor. Together with the Industrial Revolution, it introduced a structural change into Europe which sparked off developments in the state, society, economics, and law which, in turn, prepared the ground for the social evolution of the nineteenth century. It destroyed the European system of nation states that was only partially reconstructed later at the time of the Bourbon Restoration.

Fritz Novotny, in his *Painting and Sculpture in Europe: 1780–1880,* takes as his starting point the year in which Immanuel Kant completed his *Critique of Pure Reason.* Against this revolutionary event which evolved from Baroque philosophy, Novotny sets Paul Cézanne's new paintings of 1880, which marked the beginning of modern painting. K. Lankheit, in his *Revolution und Restauration,* attempts to give some idea of the revolutionary events of this age by quoting a text written by Johann Wolfgang von Goethe on October 5, 1786: "During this journey I wish to bring peace to my mind through art and its beauty, to impress its holy image right into my very soul and to guard it there for quiet enjoyment. Then, however, I will turn my attention to the work of the artisan and, on my return, take up the study of Chemistry and Mathematics. For the time of the beautiful is past; our age is the age of need and harsh necessity."

Novotny, in his discussion of art, calls this period "The Century of Naturalism," although he acknowledges the existence of contrary forces: "Never before had there been such a degree of Naturalism in painting, not even in Holland in the seventeenth century. To use 'closeness to nature' rather than Naturalism may be a little precise, but it is a more fitting description of the basic trend of nineteenth-century art. For the painting of this century was 'naturalistic' only now and again—for example, during Impressionism everywhere in Europe; but it kept close to nature even when it pursued programmes in opposition to Naturalism, such as those of Classicism and Romanticism. The element logically opposed to Naturalism, to the representation of the visible, was Idealism, that painting of ideas which occurs in many forms in the art of the nineteenth century. This Idealism, however, when it appeared in direct opposition to Naturalism, hardly ever had the same artistic strength."

In his *Abendländische Kunst* (*Art of the Western World*), Kurt Bauch gives his interpretation of post-Baroque art the heading of "Liberal Art," and places his studies in a historical setting which extends beyond the confines of art proper: "In this world of practical life, art has acquired a novel and special place. It lifts man away from sober reality and transports him into the Sunday world of the museum or of nature. In both cases this is something new. Art takes as its theme nature for its own sake."

The salon, the exhibition, the museum became in the nineteenth century the new influential meeting places for art which, in this changed society, had lost its former position. Church and castle had been deprived of their leading roles as patrons of contemporary art when the political order for which they had been responsible was broken up and disintegrated. Now museum and exhibition hall served as a formative experience for a middle class that either created for itself its own educational opportunities in order to develop its awareness as a class (through the foundation of artistic societies, for example), or had them provided by liberal-minded

ROBERT ADAM (1728–1792). Entrance hall, Syon House, Isleworth, Middlesex. 1762–69

princes (Maximilian II stated that the basic purpose of the Bavarian National Museum was to be for the honor and edification of his people).

This encouragement of the arts, however, lagged behind the evolution of the artist. In the nineteenth century, the gap widens between artist and public; progressive art stands out more and more strongly in opposition to society. The artist is forced into isolation, into a position of exception, which has its counterpart in a remarkable cult of solitude (see, for example, the representation of Mazeppa as a symbol of the artist's life in the work of Théodore Géricault, page 53).

Jacques-Louis David became the great painter of the Revolution in France. Official and progressive art come together in the large-scale Neoclassical picture. The art of the nineteenth century, however, always reflects the conflict between the official school and the opposition. Thus, official art is usually connected with traditional tendencies, frequently comes to grief in the large-scale commissioned works of monumental programs, or achieves only poor results in this sphere. There are examples of this even in David, and in Jean-Auguste-Dominique Ingres too, whose official works are inferior in quality to his portraits and free compositions.

In contrast to Ingres's *Apotheosis of Homer* (page 24), a gathering of men of genius hieratically ordered in accordance with one of the ideals of classical Antiquity, there is the great studio painting of Gustave Courbet (pages 90–91)—one of the high points of the art of the "citoyen"—which stems, in its large-scale conception, from the official salon pictures. But it has this major difference from them: instead of an immortal elite of great minds, we have here a group of friends, ordinary people of the present-day world, out of which an allegory is developed—*"une allégorie réelle,"* as Courbet designated the work. When his paintings were refused by the Salon committee of the International Exposition of 1855, Courbet protested by setting up a rival exhibition of his works in a wooden hut, an Anti-Salon.

The isolation of art into a separate realm of its own implies the possibility that it may turn in on itself. As a result, particular attention was devoted to artistic technique. Impressionism, which sought to represent the visual as a purely optical phenomenon in terms of reflected light, became in this connection a crowning artistic achievement and a turning point of great significance. The Impressionist movement stemmed from the nineteenth-century tradition of plein-air painting; at the same time, it was linked with elements of the Baroque period, as reformulated by Théodore Géricault and Eugène Delacroix during the nineteenth century. The graphic quality of color is set free as a value in its own right, independent of the objects represented. At the same time, color is no longer considered as a blending of shades but is given an independent role in its clear primary form. In the work of the Impressionists, this was still founded on illusionistic effects, but was subsequently set free as an optical element by the Pointillists in a movement that paralleled scientifically based research into optics. In this way, color is led back to itself and becomes an independent material whose laws are placed in the service of a new poetical freedom. This was the starting point for Vincent van Gogh and Paul Gauguin, who conceived color in itself as a factor in expressivity and made use of it in this way.

Just as color was liberated through being given its own meaning, so too a new formal conception of the picture was developed in the second half of the nineteenth century. Here too, the independent meaning which the Impressionists gave to the materials they used formed a turning point; new criteria evolved, and the movement reached its culmination in the work of Paul Cézanne. Historical research and historical sciences were developed methodically in the nineteenth century, and the fundamental organization which they were given still remains valid in wide areas today. This development also had an effect on the art of the period.

LEO VON KLENZE (1784–1864). Heroes' Gallery, Glyptothek (Sculpture Gallery), Munich. 1816–30. From Klenze's collection of architectural projects

8

In some cases, artists either instituted or participated in researches, with the result that their works of art were influenced by their subsequent conclusions. Architecture in particular may be quoted as an example of this; the past was used as a model, but in a different way from previously—a way calculated to draw the spectator out of prosaic, everyday reality. A longing for originality and a need for a sense of order and security that had once existed stimulated these retreats into history, into the past, to the dreams of a lost paradise.

This need provides the link between Jean-Jacques Rousseau's slogan of "back to nature," the dreams of Antiquity of the Neoclassicists, the medieval fantasies of the Romantics, and even Gauguin's Tahiti, which was followed by a love for everything "primitive" (again the search for originality) at the beginning of the present century. Whether and in what way the wide-ranging attempts at reconstruction after the Second World War are linked with a historical interest in the past will only become clear in the course of time.

In the nineteenth century, theories about art acquired a new importance. Hans von Marées's assertion that the statements he made were just as important as his pictures is typical of this. Indeed, the artistic experiments of the most recent times ("Conceptual Art") lead to a renewed interest in this aspect. Theoretical preoccupations with art (and here again, interpretation is a typical feature of the age) became a subject of study in its own right, and in the process adopted artistic principles. Any deeper study of the art of the nineteenth century involves—to a greater extent than was true for previous ages—a concern with the theories which surrounded

KLENZE. Design for a Pantechnicon in Athens. 1836.
From Klenze's collection of architectural projects

HERMANN VON DER HUDE and GEORG THEODOR SCHIRRMACHER. Kunsthalle, Hamburg. 1863–69

it. Some important potential developments only came to light by this method, never actually being put into practice.

The idea of the total work of art (*Gesamtkunstwerk*) shows how a theory which was only partially realized at the time may nevertheless contain some artistic value; and it shows, too, how many works of art can only be understood in the light of this theory. The idea of the total work of art rests on older traditions; it emerged as a lofty ideal in the nineteenth century, when the absence of unity in the arts was deeply felt. Philipp Otto Runge's reflections on this theme come to mind, or Richard Wagner's great projects, or the Romantics' idea of the *correspondance des arts,* which was formulated afresh at the time of the Symbolists. In the same way that the Romantics had striven to transform life into a total work of art, Art Nouveau devoted similar strivings toward an artistic stylization of all expressions of life and of the human environment. The Bauhaus represented similar ideas in our own era, and for that purpose—with a backward glance at the Middle Ages—took architecture as its foundation.

Even this volume appears today as a result of nineteenth-century ideas and their developments. This type of book, which is characteristic of our age and is based on a wide choice of art forms of all ages and countries, has its origins in the nineteenth century. We now have the dreams of bygone days in front of our eyes, thanks to the possibilities of photographic reproduction, in the museum of the imagination, to use André Malraux's term; and we view them as interpreters. We, that is, both readers and artists: Pablo Picasso's interpretative approach in his series of variations on the work of Cranach, Velázquez, Manet, and others comes to mind; and countless further examples could be cited.

Just as the beginning of this period of art, labeled by the chronological term "nineteenth century," can only be tentatively defined, so its end in the twentieth century still remains indeterminate. Here it runs into the art of the present day ("modern art") and is by turns repudiated by, or is acclaimed as a forerunner of, it in the ever-changing sequence of protesting avant-gardists which continues right up to the present time.

The principle of movements quickly succeeding each other, which dominates the nineteenth century, continues to apply. Again and again, a completely new art form emerges, comes into prominence, outdistances all the others, declines after a certain time because of a more modern development, and then merges into the past. The artistic experience of today has historical parallels which date back to the nineteenth century.

FRIEDRICH AUGUST STÜLER (1800–1865). Longitudinal section of staircase,
Neues Museum, Berlin. 1841–55. From Stüler's *Bauwerken* (*Buildings*), 1862

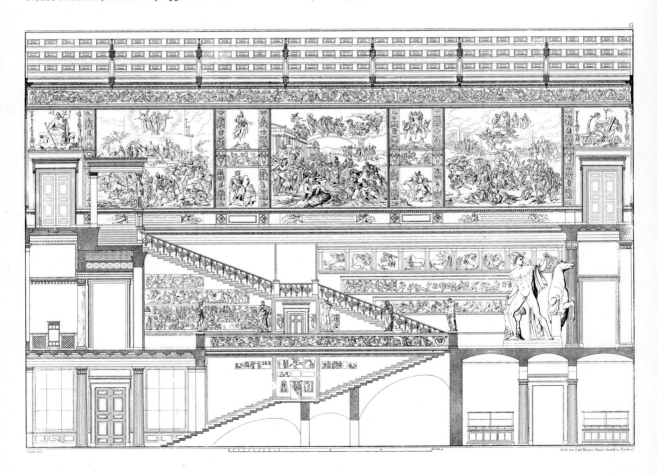

JACQUES-LOUIS DAVID (1748–1825). *The Oath of the Horatii*. 1784. Oil on canvas, 10′ 10″ × 14′. The Louvre, Paris

PAINTING

Jacques-Louis David's *The Oath of the Horatii* ranks as the most important formative work of early Neo-classicism. It was painted in Paris, after the artist's visit to Rome, when Louis XVI was still on the throne. The relief-like composition, the groups of parallel figures, and the cool, sharp light which gives a limpid metallic effect all distinguish the picture from the Baroque concepts of art. It was defined by a moralizing pathos, in the formation of which the lines and the sculptured modeling of the figures gain a new significance. The graphic values of Baroque—and David was influenced by the imprint given to it by the French classicist painter Nicolas Poussin—are replaced by classical clarity for which archetypes were sought in ancient art. This severity of form, the content of which was intended to have a moral import for the viewer, accords with the philosophy of enlightenment of the French Revolution of 1789, whose ideals David actively supported.

DAVID. *The Death of Marat.* 1793. Oil on canvas, 63³/₄ × 50³/₈″. Musées Royaux des Beaux-Arts de Belgique, Brussels

David became a Jacobin. As a member of the National Convention he organized state support for the arts, but after the fall of Robespierre he was put on trial and hourly expected death himself. In paintings of political martyrs, he extolled the heroes of the Revolution. If with his *Oath of the Horatii* David had produced the manifesto of Neoclassical art, with the representation of the murdered Marat he formulated a new approach to the heroic picture which set new standards with its simplified composition. Different traditions from religious and secular painting were brought together into a new creative form by the artist, committed as he was to the ideals of the Revolution. The ideological force of conviction of this work was never again achieved, even by David himself.

David's paintings of ancient history sought parallels in the past for contemporary events, and they were understood in this way at the time. When the picture on the facing page was exhibited in the Salon of 1789, the Bastille had been stormed and the States General convened. It was taken as a symbol of an approaching era of harsh political inflexibility.

DAVID. *The Lictors Bringing to Brutus the Bodies of His Sons* (detail). 1789. Oil on canvas, 10′ 8″ × 14′. The Louvre, Paris ▶

DAVID. *Napoleon Crossing the Great St. Bernard Pass*. 1800.
Oil on canvas, 8′ 8″ × 7′ 7″. Kunsthistorisches Museum, Vienna

Napoleon appointed David his court painter. While he continued painting scenes from ancient history, he also paid tribute to the idolized leader with paintings based on the history of Napoleon's Consulate and Empire. In these works one can see the danger signs of a limp and rather colorless stylized painting. Even the Vienna work (facing page) remains first and foremost an instructive historical monument, and lacks the noble conviction of the *Marat*.

David's portraits are free of the twin dangers of the Neoclassicists' imitation of the ancients and idealization of contemporary events. In them his outstanding talent is displayed in its greatest clarity and freedom. In the portrait of Madame Récamier, the color, which is subordinated to the severe composition, is loosely applied in a thin layer of pigment within the clear outline of the figure. The lady portrayed, the wife of a Paris banker, was a popular society beauty and wit, and her salon was the meeting place of the notables of the day. The piece of furniture—*"le lit à l'antique"*— on which she is reclining in the picture became famous in its own right: it was made from designs by David and his pupil Moreau.

DAVID. *Portrait of Madame Récamier*. Started 1800, unfinished. Oil on canvas, $68^1/_8 \times 95^5/_8''$. The Louvre, Paris

GROS. *Napoleon at Arcole*. 1796. Oil on canvas, 28³/₄ × 23¹/₄″. The Louvre, Paris

After the restoration of the Bourbons in 1816 David was forced to leave France, and he took up residence in Brussels. However, his great influence had founded an important school of painters, of which Antoine-Jean Gros was the most outstanding member. When he was only fourteen years old, he had begun to work under David. His monumental picture *Napoleon at Eylau* (facing page) is an important example of the genre of battlefield scenes, which became Gros's specialty. This old tradition in painting was given fresh impetus by the Napoleonic campaigns at that time, and through the link with the cult of Napoleon became exaggerated to a portrayal of the near-superhuman. Patriotism and hero worship became the dominant themes of pictorial art, as can be seen from the innumerable series of contemporary printed reproductions of this type of picture.

François-Pascal
Gérard (1770–1837).
*Portrait of Madame
Récamier*. 1802. Oil
on canvas, 88⅝ ×
57⅛″. Musée Carna-
valet, Paris

Among David's pupils, François-Pascal Gérard was the closest to his master, but he modified David's grandiose sense of pathos with an intellectually tempered sensitivity. His talent as "an amiable classicist" (Novotny) was shown at its best in portrait painting. The portrait of Madame Récamier on the facing page is an outstanding illustration of this. The classical clarity of David's masterpiece (page 17) is especially striking in comparison with Gérard's work, which was a friendlier, more intimate approach in its attempt to reflect the charm of this much admired lady. The portrait is more sumptuous and outward-going in its effect than is David's somewhat reserved painting. In place of David's elemental simplicity, Gérard's picture has an animation which spills over into decorativeness, recalling the traditions of the Rococo era.

The contemporary public preferred the more intimate style of Gérard to the progressive art of David. Instead of revolutionary power and the bourgeois ideals of enlightenment, they preferred the reconstruction of the more playful life of the Rococo courts. This charming portrait of Madame Récamier achieved greater renown than David's austere masterpiece, and the latter's importance for the future went unrecognized. The terra-cotta statuette of Madame Récamier illustrates this very clearly. It shows the influence of Gérard's portrait and follows the original in all important details. Even more clearly than the painting, the delicate Rococo tradition can be seen in this typical example of the sculptural miniatures of the period. The fine quality of this essentially visual work is not dissipated in frivolity, despite all its lightheartedness.

Pierre-Paul Prud'hon arrived in Rome when David was at the height of his renown there. More important in their influence on Prud'hon, however, were Canova and the Renaissance masters Raphael and (as the example opposite shows) Leonardo and Correggio. His unique use of silver-gray lighting was to be important for Corot's later works.

Jean-Auguste-Dominique Ingres, the last of the great French Neoclassical painters, became David's pupil at the age of seventeen, and his creative period extended from the early years of the century up to the beginnings of Impressionism. He followed his teacher in the treatment of form as a classical problem. Ingres's skill in drawing also underlies his paintings, in which his remarkable realism of detail and his selective application of color enable him to evolve from the classical principles of form a unique effect of perspective on the flat surface of the picture. David had not achieved this effect, and it earns Ingres a special position in nineteenth-century painting. By his new treatment of color, Ingres moved away from David's precepts. Together with the art of Antiquity, he took as his model the paintings of the High Renaissance, especially those of Raphael.

The Apotheosis of Homer (see page 24), came to stand as a declaration of modern beliefs. The picture is an artistic and literary credo of the painter: around Homer are grouped the poets, painters, and musicians

INGRES. *The Apotheosis of Homer.* 1827. Oil on
canvas, 12′ 8″ × 16′ 10³/₄″. The Louvre, Paris

who pay him homage—their selection reflecting the taste of the day. Raphael and Dante stand to the right
of Homer, raised up among the ranks of the artists of Antiquity. The appearance of Shakespeare among the
moderns in the foreground is interesting, since his later influence on the Romantics was to be so great.

Ingres's principle ran: every great graphic artist finds the exact color to correspond to the outline he has
drawn. In this way he made visual coherence the basis of his art, just as Cézanne approached the problem
from the opposite direction, that of color. The harmonious color tones of *Les Grandes Baigneuses* (page 151)
are paralleled in the clear, simple composition of the picture, which, in contrast to Ingres's and David's work,
creates rectilinear lines of tension on the three-dimensional perspective of the painting.

INGRES. *The Bather of Valpinçon.* 1808. Oil ▶
on canvas, 56³/₄ × 38¹/₈″. The Louvre, Paris

24

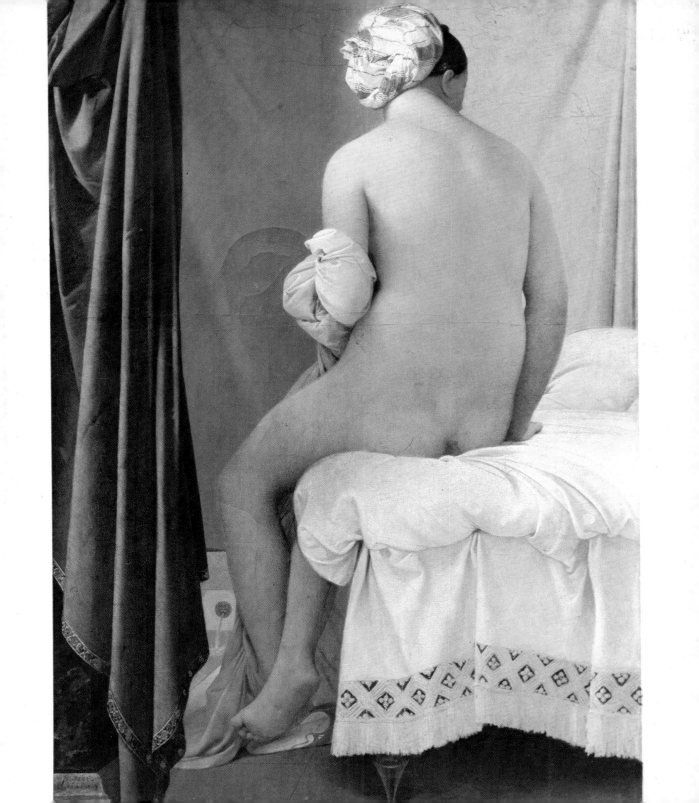

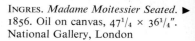

INGRES. *Madame Moitessier Seated.*
1856. Oil on canvas, 47$^{1}/_{4}$ × 36$^{1}/_{4}$".
National Gallery, London

INGRES. *Joan of Arc at the Corona-tion of Charles VII.* 1854. Oil on canvas, 94$^{1}/_{2}$ × 70$^{1}/_{8}$". The Louvre, Paris

The work of Ingres is deeply penetrated by themes from history and the vigor of his severe classical compo-sition bestows upon his paintings their heroic grandeur. The liveliness of the tonal values and the realism in the portrayal of details make even themes from the past become real in his paintings, skillfully combining an artistic design with an insistent clarity of expression.

A quality of perfection belongs essentially to the art of Ingres and embodies the highest refinement of balance in outline, form, and tonal representation. This combination attracted numerous later artists —among them Puvis de Chavannes, Degas, and Renoir. With all their orderliness in the main details, the psychological depth and authenticity of his portraits are amazing. The portrait of Mme. Moitessier (facing page) represents a high point in the work of the artist, who was seventy-six years old at the time. The rich, powerful interplay of local coloring is subordinated in an abundant variety of ways to the clarity of the general composition.

The early years of the German Neoclassicists lack the magnificent power of conviction of the French painters of the David school. The art of Anton Raphael Mengs and Asmus Jakob Carstens exemplifies this turning away from the Baroque to the new endeavors of the nineteenth century. Carstens was strongly influenced by the writings of Karl Ludwig Fernow and—stimulated by the theories of this man—developed his own art of pure outline, under the influence of Antiquity (especially Greek painted vases), from Raphael and Michelangelo. The drawing in the Hamburg Kunsthalle shows the artist who died when still young, his high artistic promise denied the opportunity of full realization.

Christian Gottlieb Schick belongs to the generation of artists through whom Neoclassical art extended its sphere of influence in Germany. He studied from 1798 to 1802 in David's studio and before that time had already come indirectly into contact with French Neoclassicism through Hetsch, his Stuttgart teacher. Some of his portraits, in particular, can be placed alongside the French portraits of David and his school as characteristic products of a typical example of German Neoclassicism.

CHRISTIAN GOTTLIEB SCHICK (1776–1812). *Wilhelmine von Cotta.* 1802. Oil on canvas, 52 × 55¹/₈″. Staatsgalerie, Stuttgart

Joseph Anton Koch's canvases mark the crowning point of German Neoclassical landscape painting. For this son of a Tyrolean peasant, the experience of the Alps was decisive, and their overpowering influence led to moral comparisons in Koch's art, which thus shows an affinity with the moral and descriptive Swiss landscape poetry of Albrecht von Haller (*Die Alpen*, 1729) and Salomon Gessner (*Idyllen*, 1756), and with Goethe's description of the Swiss Alps. The fundamental idea is the relationship between human form and

landscape. With a unity of formation and execution which is preserved down to the last detail, Koch sought to embody in his pictures the significance and the poetic ideas which he felt were implicit in a landscape. The clear, classical articulation of his painting betrays the definite influence of Poussin, the basic elements of whose art —Arcadian figures, motifs of classical architecture, and a clearly perceptible depth of spatial perspective— were given fresh form by Koch.

WILHELM VON KOBELL (1766–1853). *Huntsman on the Hochalm.* 1828. Oil on canvas, 15$^1/_8$ × 13$^1/_8$″. Schäfer Collection, Schweinfurt

The art of Wilhelm von Kobell belongs to the tradition of classical landscape painting, and at the same time his work shows some similarity to the objective clarity of Biedermeier realism, as is typified most strikingly by Ferdinand Georg Waldmüller. From his father Ferdinand came the influence of Dutch seventeenth-century painting, especially that of the Italianate painters of the Netherlands, whose works forecast Kobell's special interest in lighting. From the Neoclassicists he derived the idea of rigorous pictorial composition and the sharpened outline of distant objects; in the cool light, these outlines assume the enchanted form of a still life and the construction of the picture has the static quality of an architectural structure.

◀ JOSEPH ANTON KOCH (1768–1839). *Heroic Landscape with Rainbow.* 1805. Oil on canvas, 45$^7/_8$ × 44$^1/_4$″. Staatliche Kunsthalle, Karlsruhe

In contrast to Koch's organized landscape painting, which portrays the grandeur of the natural world in which man is still at home, boundless expanses of space predominate in Caspar David Friedrich's landscapes. They offer no resting place to man, but express a certain trembling sense of awe. Nature becomes a partner in a romantic dialogue and comes to represent a religious theme. Landscape painting, which originated around 1600, was given a new impetus by this emotional formulation of the Romantics.

CASPAR DAVID FRIEDRICH (1774–1840). *The Cross in the Mountains (Tetschen Altar)*. 1808. Painted for the private chapel of Count Thun. Oil on canvas, 45¼ × 43¼". Staatliche Kunstsammlungen, Dresden

FRIEDRICH. *Ship in the Arctic*. 1798. Oil on canvas, 11⅝ × 8⅝". Kunsthalle, Hamburg ▶

Carl Gustav Carus, Johan Christian Clausen Dahl, and Friedrich Georg Kersting are the chief representatives of the group of artists who worked with Friedrich, the Dresden Romantic. Carus—physicist, doctor, and philosopher—is closest to Friedrich in his interpretation of nature. From him, Carus adopted the motif of the figure turning away, a key to the Romantic dialogue with the world in landscape painting. His writings won him a reputation as the most significant theorist of Romantic landscape art.

CARL GUSTAV CARUS (1789–1869). *Window on the Oybin by Moonlight.* c. 1828. Oil on canvas, 10³/₄ × 12¹/₂″. Georg Schäfer Collection, Obbach

JOHAN CHRISTIAN CLAUSEN DAHL (1788–1857). *Eruption of Vesuvius.* 1826. Oil on canvas, 50³/₈ × 67³/₄″. Städelsches Kunstinstitut, Frankfurt am Main

The Norwegian Dahl spent a large part of his life in Dresden, and although he was influenced considerably by Friedrich, he developed beyond the latter's art. Through his special and practical interest in light and atmosphere Dahl became one of the founders of realism in landscape painting. Apart from Friedrich and earlier Scandinavian forerunners, he was also influenced by Dutch painting of the seventeenth century.

FRIEDRICH GEORG KERSTING (1785–1847). *Caspar David Friedrich in His Studio.* 1811. Oil on canvas, 21¹/₄ × 16¹/₂″. Kunsthalle, Hamburg ▶

Kersting was not a landscape painter. Nevertheless, his typical scenes of interiors give this genre a new imprint, the mood of which seems to bear some relationship to the landscape paintings of Friedrich.

If Friedrich represents the most important landscape painter of the Romantic period, Philipp Otto Runge ranks with him as the figure painter of the time. In his picture of *Morning* (page 37), of which there are several versions, Runge endeavors to overcome this division between landscape painting and figure painting. His ideal was a work of art which should combine the two, in which both nature and the human figure should carry the message, the one being supported by the other.

The union of landscape and figures was brought to perfection by the following generation of Romantics, the so-called Nazarenes. Under the direction of Johann Friedrich Overbeck and Franz Pforr, this group of German painters went to Rome in 1810 and sought out new sources of inspiration there, having left the Vienna Academy out of dissatisfaction with its teaching. In so doing, Pforr decided to turn back to German art of the past and sought out scenes from medieval history and legends for his themes.

CARL PHILIPP FOHR (1795–1818). *Landscape with Shepherds.* 1817. Oil on canvas, 38⅝ × 53⅛″. Collection Prince von Hessen und zu Rhein, Darmstadt

Carl Philipp Fohr arrived in Rome in 1816 and joined forces with the Nazarenes. The influence of Koch was decisive for him. In this period at the beginning of the nineteenth century, with its diverse experiments in new directions, Fohr plays an important role. His landscape is neither a picture with a meaning, as with Friedrich, nor is it a heroic landscape suffused with poetry, as in the case of Koch. To the beauty of the coloring and of the figures with their open countenances there corresponds an over-all mood which accords more with the here and now—in contrast to Friedrich's dream worlds and Koch's powerful compositions— though its cheerfulness betrays a touch of Romantic melancholy.

◀ FRANZ PFORR (1788–1812). *Rudolf of Habsburg and the Priest.* c. 1809. Oil on canvas, 18 × 21½″. Städelsches Kunstinstitut, Frankfurt am Main

JOHANN FRIEDRICH OVERBECK (1789–1869). *The Triumph of Religion in the Arts*. 1840. Oil on canvas, 11′ 1¹⁄₂″ × 12′ 9¹⁄₂″. Städelsches Kunstinstitut, Frankfurt am Main

Overbeck, together with Pforr and other painters, founded the *Lukasbruderschaft* (Brotherhood of St. Luke) in Vienna, even before they migrated to Rome to live and work there together as "Nazarenes." *The Triumph of Religion in the Arts* clearly shows Overbeck's debt to Raphael, the pattern of whose art he attempted to follow. At the same time, the painting above (commissioned by the Städelsches Kunstinstitut) speaks powerfully of the Nazarene philosophy, of their dream of an order of society oriented toward the Middle Ages, in which the Catholic Church brings together all men as believers and art itself finds its highest purpose and its immortality in the service of religion.

During his stay in Italy in the years 1827–29, Joseph von Führich, too, joined the Nazarenes and under the direction of Overbeck worked together with Koch, Julius Schnorr von Carolsfeld, and Philipp Veit on the frescoes at the Villa Massimo. His work is in the main devoted to religious art and his representation of "pious calm" seeks to portray peace and harmony. In artistic temperament he is at the opposite pole to Peter von Cornelius (see page 44). In this respect, along with Raphael and the other painters of the High Renaissance, the gentle world of Fra Angelico had an important influence on him.

JOSEPH VON FÜHRICH (1800–1876). *The Road To Emmaus.* 1837. Oil on canvas, 11³/₈ × 17³/₈″. Kunsthalle, Bremen

JULIUS SCHNORR VON CAROLSFELD (1794–1872). *The Battle of the Knights on Lipadusa.* 1816. After Ariosto, *Orlando Furioso,* 41–42. Oil on canvas, 40 × 67″. Kunsthalle, Bremen

Schnorr von Carolsfeld, who came to Rome in 1818 and likewise joined forces with the Nazarenes, had previously studied at the Vienna Academy and was a pupil of Koch and Ferdinand Olivier. In the develop- ment of his work, his feeling for large-scale composition shows itself ever more strongly, leading him to undertake numerous cycles of fresco painting. *The Battle of the Knights on Lipadusa* is the earliest example of Schnorr's painting that we have, dating from before his stay in Italy. The interpretation of the literary theme —Roland's victory over the Saracens—as a struggle between the pagan world (on the left) and Christianity (on the right) shows already at this early date Schnorr's special talent for monumental painting.

Ferdinand Olivier, the most important landscape artist of the Nazarene school, never went to Italy. His painting of the Holy Family dates from the time when he and his brother Heinrich were in Vienna, where they met, and learned from, Koch, Schnorr von Carolsfeld, and other artists. He had previously studied under Eichen-Kolbe and had spent some time with Friedrich's group in Dresden. Friedrich influenced him strongly, but the dramatic qualities of Friedrich's landscapes do not feature in the work of Olivier; Koch had an even stronger influence, but his heroic elements are absent here. Olivier's paintings bear the imprint of a clear straightforwardness, with which he gives expression to the Nazarene ideal of medieval simplicity without losing credibility by too slavish an imitation.

FERDINAND OLIVIER (1785–1841). *Landscape with the Holy Family and John the Baptist.* 1824. Oil on wood, $8^{3}/_{8} \times 12^{1}/_{2}''$. Folkwang Museum, Essen

Peter von Cornelius went to Italy in 1811 and joined the Nazarene group. His early work—twelve illustrations for Goethe's *Faust* and seven for the *Nibelungenlied*—sets him apart most clearly from the work of his fellow Nazarenes. In spite of a delicate sense of line and of modeling, the powerful over-all impression is here astonishingly bold in contrast to the tender emotional pattern of the Nazarenes' work, expressed at its gentlest by Führich. An important guide for Cornelius was the graphic art of Dürer, in which the most mannered aspects particularly appealed to him. Bizarre elements already found their way into his early work, becoming more and more pronounced in his Roman paintings. The frescoes commissioned for the Munich Glyptothek confronted Cornelius with classical themes, and resulted in a development toward Neoclassicism, to which the painter remained faithful from then on.

PETER VON CORNELIUS (1783–1867). *Faust and Mephistopheles on the Rabenstein*. 1814. Copper engraving, $15^3/_8 \times 20^1/_4''$

ALFRED RETHEL (1816–1859). *Death on Horseback*. From
The Dance of Death, plate 6. 1849. Woodcut, $8^3/_4 \times 12^1/_2''$

Alfred Rethel, who was a generation younger than Cornelius, carried on in the tradition of the historical
picture but gave it a new meaning (as the Nazarene had done in his own special way). In place of the
idealizing works of Schnorr, Cornelius, and Wilhelm von Kaulbach, contemporary history is given form here,
especially in *The Dance of Death*—a set of scenes of revolution which are among Rethel's best-known
work, and in which he was able to combine realistic representation and allegorical meaning in a unique way.

Francisco José de Goya y Lucientes was a contemporary of the Neoclassicists. His art, however, stands in complete contrast to that of David, Blake, Fuseli, and Runge: it originates in the Late Baroque tradition. The demonic element which is an essential part of it does not accord with Neoclassical enlightenment and can only be compared with similar expressions in contemporary music and poetry (Beethoven, Goethe). The demonic appears in the work of Goya not as a morally considered opposite to good, not as a spectral vision, but in daily life, in the faces of men, and in the terrors of war. Goya took themes from Tiepolo and Velázquez —the two chief sources of his inspiration. From Tiepolo comes the great dramatic portrayal of Baroque dynamism, of which *The Third of May, 1808* is a particularly fine example. From Velázquez there came the vital stimulus for Goya's portraits; the deep understanding of human life he shows in them represents one of the high points in the art of the portrait. The supple freedom of the brushwork and the vivid use of color place his work far above its Baroque origins and already herald the Impressionist possibilities of the second half of the nineteenth century.

Francisco José de Goya y Lucientes (1746–1828). *The Third of May, 1808*. 1814. Oil on canvas, 8′ 8″ × 11′ 4″. The Prado, Madrid

GOYA. *Queen Maria Luisa of Spain.* 1798. Oil on canvas, $82^1/_4 \times 49^1/_4''$. The Prado, Madrid

GOYA. *An Accident that Occurred in the Ringside Seats of the Madrid Arena, and the Death of the Mayor of Torrejon.* From *Tauromaquia*, plate 21. 1815. Etching, $8^1/_4 \times 12^1/_2''$

Goya's masterly series of etchings are among the most significant works in this art form, and they provide numerous insights into the way in which this artist-genius perceived the world. Goya's graphic art would have been impossible without the etchings of Rembrandt; and the graphic art of Tiepolo and Jacques Callot was also an important influence. The *Tauromaquia* is a description of the techniques and rules of the bullfight and of the important episodes in its history, but its apparent objectivity shades into criticism and denunciation of the sport.

GOYA. *Saturn Devouring His Children.* c. 1815. Oil on canvas, $57\frac{1}{2} \times 32\frac{5}{8}''$. The Prado, Madrid

When Théodore Géricault, the first great painter of the French Romantic school, died in 1824 at the age of thirty-two, David was still alive, and many of the distinctive features of Géricault's art would have been unthinkable without him. Nevertheless, important elements in Géricault's work stem from the Baroque tradition, and this links him with Goya. The striking visual impact of the mounted officer, the splendid artistry in

JEAN-LOUIS-ANDRÉ-THÉODORE GÉRICAULT (1791–1824). *Mounted Officer of the Imperial Guard.* 1812. Oil on canvas, 9′ 7″ × 6′ 4³/₈″. The Louvre, Paris

GÉRICAULT. *The Madwoman* (from a series of paintings of the mentally deranged). 1822–23. Oil on canvas, 28³/₈ × 22⁷/₈″. Musée des Beaux-Arts, Lyons

the handling of color, hark back to the Baroque and at the same time give a good example of Géricault's unique position among the artists of his day, denoting the onset of a new trend which was to reach its highest achievement with Delacroix and which had a profound effect on the early years of modern painting in the second half of the nineteenth century. Géricault strove passionately to bring realism into his art, evidence of which is to be seen with particular starkness in his paintings of executed criminals and madmen.

The story of the young Polish courtier Mazeppa was often depicted in the nineteenth century—especially in the work of the French Romantic school. In addition to Géricault, renderings by Delacroix, Boulanger, Vernet, and Chassériau have also survived. Mazeppa, tied naked to a horse, became a symbol and an interpretation of the sufferings of the artist—of the man of genius who endures so much for the sake of his art.

The large-scale painting (16′ 1″ x 23′ 6″) of which this is a preliminary study refers to a contemporary event. It is justly considered to be the manifesto of the new post-David school of painting. However, its moral intention, its conception, as well as the formality of its execution originate from the teaching of David, and remind us of the epic scope of Gros's battlefield scenes. In matters of form Géricault brings together the Baroque diagonal composition and the pyramidal construction of the Neoclassical school. The result of his penetrating and detailed studies of models, of survivors of the catastrophe, of corpses in the hospital, and of a copy of the raft of the "Medusa" enables him in his art to move away from the traditional methods already mentioned and to set new standards.

GÉRICAULT. *The Raft of the "Medusa"* (preliminary study). c. 1818. Oil and pen on canvas, 25⁵/₈ × 32⁵/₈″. The Louvre, Paris

Delacroix is the authoritative artist of the so-
called Romantic school, an artistic movement
in France which can only be partially related
to the earlier Romantic movement in Germany, although Delacroix himself did have
connections with the German Romantics.
His typical preference for scenes full of pas-
sion goes directly back to Géricault and
through him to the great inheritance of the
Baroque period—especially Rubens—and
of the Renaissance—especially Veronese.
More than any other artist of his time, he
also studied works from the most diverse
periods—from Antiquity through the Middle
Ages right up to his own day—and extracted
from them ideas for the complex formation
of his own artistic style. His pictures come to
life in their coloring. As a painter in the
Baroque tradition, he was the foremost representative of the followers of Rubens, as
opposed to the followers of Poussin, among
whom Ingres was the greatest. Numerous
works of Delacroix take their inspiration
from literary topics. A leading work of his
early period resulted, however, from the impression made by a contemporary event, the
July Revolution of 1830. The moral import
of the scene can be compared with the political paintings of David, but there is here a
new sense of passionate feeling—in the
manner of Géricault's *Raft of the "Medusa"*
—with a strong sense of realism.

54

DELACROIX. *Women of Algiers.* 1834. Oil on
canvas, 69⅝ × 89⅜″. The Louvre, Paris

Despite the veneration he had for the art of Antiquity and the eager study that he devoted to it, Delacroix
visited neither Italy nor Greece. An important event for him was the journey which—as a member of a
political mission—he made to Algeria in 1832. According to his own report, he came across the world of
Antiquity there in a living form. From his trip he brought back a large number of studies and paintings together with many ideas for later works. The Algerian experience also extended his range of color—Delacroix

was deeply influenced by the dazzling appearance of the world in the strong sunlight of this foreign land —and this brought out more fully in the artist qualities which he had already put to use in his early work. *Women of Algiers,* a picture that gave Delacroix's successors—from Renoir to Matisse—vital inspiration, is a good example of the influence. His artistry raises this painting far above the general run of works that resulted from the contemporary craze for the Oriental.

The violent dynamics reminiscent of the Baroque period and the graphic representation of the brute strength which develops in the struggle between beasts and men, also typical of Delacroix's art, may be seen at their clearest in the various versions of the lion-hunt theme. Here, he has much in common with Rubens. The painting below is noteworthy for its special use of color, in which the role of the colors as a factor in the creation of movement begins to assert its hegemony over figures and objects, a technique which looks back to the Baroque tradition but also forward to the characteristic features of the Impressionists.

DELACROIX. *Lion Hunt.* c. 1860. Oil on canvas, 27³/₈ × 40¹/₄″. Kunsthalle, Bremen

DELACROIX. *Jacob Wrestling with the Angel* (detail). 1856–61. Mural, left wall, Chapelle des Anges, Saint-Sulpice, Paris

The wall paintings at Saint-Sulpice come at the end of the series of large-scale mural decorations which Delacroix carried out in the course of his career. Completed two years before the death of the artist, once again they represent in monumental form the composite statement of his art. What is more, his important recognition, which was to have far-reaching effects, that color is, above all, light and that shadows consist of reflections of color, is here expressed on an immense scale; complex ideas and intense observation are balanced against each other and are here given form in a way which at that time was unique.

"Delacroix occupies so prominent a position, not because he is the greatest artist in color of all time, but because he made color into a complete organic expression of his mind. It is not his great affection for the Old Masters which establishes his claim to fame but the effectiveness of this love, the insertion of values of the Old Masters into the bloodstream of contemporary creation. Nor does his passionate feeling for nature deserve any special acclaim. Ingres's naturalism was just as wholehearted a commitment, Constable's landscape art and the honesty of Runge and Friedrich were in every way as commendable. ... Only the man who is able to produce that which belongs to nature from within himself will, by depicting nature, gain the highest success" (J. Meier-Graefe).

DELACROIX. *Heliodorus Driven from the Temple* (detail). 1856–61. Mural, right wall, Chapelle des Anges, Saint-Sulpice, Paris

THÉODORE CHASSÉRIAU (1819–1856). *The Tepidarium.* 1853. Oil on canvas, 5′ 7³/₈″ × 8′ 5⁵/₈″. The Louvre, Paris

Théodore Chassériau stands midway between Ingres, whose pupil he was, and Delacroix. He is to be counted as one of the most important representatives of French *romantisme*. The graphic clarity of Ingres is allied in his work to a visual exquisiteness in the tradition of Delacroix, and both these aspects are suffused with an air of sultry, exotic sensuality.

Charles Méryon, from an early date in his artistic career, devoted himself exclusively to engraving, being color-blind. His famous set of studies *Eaux-fortes sur Paris,* which was followed by other prints of Parisian life, shows above all the menacing aspect of the city, where humans emerge as small insect-like beings. Méryon, a hypersensitive artist who died at the Charenton asylum, heightened the Romantic gloom so typical of the age into a melancholic representation of an anguished way of living, in which the Romantic demonic element is intermingled with an almost Surrealist clarity.

CHARLES MÉRYON (1821–1868). *Rue des Chantres.* 1862. Etching, 8 × 5³/₄″. Kunsthalle, Bremen

English painting, especially in the work of John Constable, made an important contribution to the development of European art. The exhibition of Constable's paintings in the Paris Salon of 1824 had a revolutionary impact; Delacroix was so impressed that he immediately painted over the background to his *Massacre at Chios* which was on exhibition at the time. Apart from the English landscape painters, Constable had also studied the work of Ruisdael and Claude Lorrain, but he soon broke free of their influence. He gave a direct and simple rendering of the landscape of his home country in its changing patterns of light and atmosphere. The penetrating study of nature that enabled him to paint in this way also found permanent expression in 1821–22 in a series of "cloudscapes" which are based on very close observation of atmospheric phenomena. Constable's large-scale landscape works, painted in the studio, made him into one of the forerunners of the Barbizon school. In their luminous, sketchlike technique, they already herald, in some way, certain characteristics of the Impressionist school.

CONSTABLE. *Clouds.* 1822. Oil on canvas, $11^3/_4$ × $19^1/_4''$. National Gallery of Victoria, Melbourne

"Painting is a science," John Constable said in 1836, and he demanded that it should be carried on like research into the natural laws. Why, he then asked, should landscape painting not be considered as a branch of natural philosophy in which paintings represent experiments? Constable turned away from the florid painting of his day and attempted by means of his pictures, which he called "experiments" to begin once more to tap the springs of simplicity. He insisted that the landscape artist must walk through the fields in all humbleness and that it was never granted to an arrogant man to see nature in all her beauty. This candid and simple view of art was developed by Constable into a new principle: whenever he sat down in the presence of nature in order to make a sketch, then first and foremost he must endeavor to forget that he had ever seen a painting.

◀ JOHN CONSTABLE (1776–1837). *Flatford Mill.* 1817. Oil on canvas, 40 × 50″. Tate Gallery, London

Benjamin West was born in Springfield, Pa., but his main activity took place in England. In the history of art he will be chiefly remembered for his early depiction of historical scenes, which, especially in his use of uniforms and ceremonial dress, opened up new areas for nineteenth-century painters. His art freed itself from the Baroque type of composition and anticipated paths that the Romantics were to explore.

BENJAMIN WEST (1738–1820). *Death of the Chevalier Bayard.* 1772. Oil on canvas, 87$^1/_4$ × 70$^1/_2$″. Kensington Palace, London

JOSEPH MALLORD WILLIAM TURNER (1775–1851). *Rain, Steam, and Speed.* 1844. Oil on canvas, 35⁷/₈ × 48″. National Gallery, London

Joseph Mallord William Turner's fantasies in color, shot through with light, have their origins in watercolor painting. These paintings, typical of his work, give an effect of transparent colorings in the hazy atmosphere where the outlines of objects are everywhere indistinct. The potential forces of color acquire a general existence of their own, independent of the objects depicted. Mood is determined by colors which, in details and as a complex whole, are intended to arouse special emotional reactions. The factor which was essential for the Impressionists of a realistic bright color based on observation of nature is lacking in the Romantic, dream-like visions of Turner. Instead, he sought to develop and enhance their sensual and moral qualities through his preoccupations with color theory.

From Barbizon, a village on the edge of the forest of Fontainebleau, there originated about the middle of the nineteenth century a new movement in landscape painting, the *paysage intime*—a form of simple, emotive portrayal of nature. The Barbizon school represents an important step forward in nineteenth-century plein-air painting, which reaches its culmination with the Impressionists. Théodore Rousseau's works are noteworthy for a special sense of pathos. To some extent, the influence of Constable may be detected in them. He is considered to be the real discoverer of this countryside, although Camille Corot, Théodore Aligny, and others had been working there for some time already.

CHARLES-FRANÇOIS DAUBIGNY (1817–1878). *The Banks of the Oise.* 1862. Oil on wood, 10¹/₄ × 22″. Musée de Reims

PIERRE-ÉTIENNE-THÉODORE ROUSSEAU (1812–1867). *The Little Fisherman.* c. 1848–49. Oil on canvas, 8¹/₈ × 12″. The Louvre, Paris

Charles-François Daubigny pursued the aims of the Barbizon school to their logical conclusion. Light and atmosphere take on in his work a new function, that characteristic quality which assumes great importance for the Impressionists. Color becomes the chief method by which form is created. Yet even in the free form of his later paintings, Daubigny does not go far beyond the ground covered by the great Dutch landscape artists.

Jean-François Millet, who belonged to the school of Barbizon, did not often paint pure landscape, for he wanted his art to serve as the pictorial representation of complex ideas about mankind and its fate. At that time, these works which exalt the life of the peasants into examples of morality, religion, and aesthetics made a deep impression on the public, and even later on Jozef Israels, Max Liebermann, Giovanni Segantini, and Vincent van Gogh. Taken in general, the art of Millet also poses certain unsolved problems. This is especially true because his main works appeared at a time when Gustave Courbet, with his realistic paintings, had found more straightforward ways of portraying simple life.

JEAN-FRANÇOIS MILLET (1814–1875). *The Gleaners.*
1857. Oil on canvas, 21 × 43³/₄″. The Louvre, Paris

JEAN-BAPTISTE-CAMILLE COROT (1796–1875). *View of the Colosseum.*
1826. Oil on paper on canvas, 11 × 18⅞". The Louvre, Paris

During Corot's first stay in Italy in the years 1825–28, he produced a series of landscape paintings depicting Rome and its surroundings, in which the gentle gradations of bright color create an artistic equivalent to the enchantment of the light and of the atmospheric mood. These works, which bring the genre of small-scale landscape art to a high point of perfection, are part of the movement of landscape painting informed by a study of nature which, from Constable, extends over Northern Europe and Germany, reaching as far as the Austrian Biedermeier painters. Corot stands at the head of this widespread development, the new pictorial powers of which owe much to the many studies in color which, up to that time, had been considered only of minor importance. The easy, sketchlike style of the small study is changed here into an open, independent expressivity; Corot's painting, by his use of the pictorial qualities of color, gives expression to a complex form which strikes the viewer as a reflection of nature and a portrayal of the values inherent in it. Among the forerunners of Impressionism, Corot—as far as color is concerned—made the greatest advance with these early paintings.

COROT. *Sens Cathedral.* 1874. Oil on canvas, 24 × 15³/₄″.
The Louvre, Paris

COROT. *Rest Beneath Willows by the Waterside.* 1865–70.
Oil on canvas, 17³/₄ × 23³/₄″. The Louvre, Paris

From his middle period onward, Corot created another type of landscape painting in which the calm of perfect harmony—a goal that greatly preoccupied the nineteenth century—becomes manifest. These landscapes bathed in silvery light depict Arcadia with its nymphs and shepherds. In contrast to his famous topographical studies, they portray an imaginary world and, despite the figures, no action is retold in the pictures. They have the effect of a lyrical theme in color which is all represented on a particular tonal level.

Sens Cathedral, one of Corot's later works, is a case of particular interest. It reminds one by its theme and its gray tonality of the specialist paintings of the Dutch school, indicating one source from which Corot's distinctive sense for color was derived.

FRIEDRICH VON AMER-
LING (1803–1887). *Ru-
dolf von Arthaber and
His Children.* 1837.
Oil on canvas, 87 ×
61". Österreichische
Galerie, Vienna

FERDINAND GEORG
WALDMÜLLER (1793
–1865). *Wolfgang-
see.* 1835. Oil on
wood, $12^3/_8$ × $10^1/_4$".
Österreichische Ga-
lerie, Vienna

Ferdinand Georg
Waldmüller is an
outstanding ex-
ample of the way
in which the Bie-
dermeier painters
gave form to nat-
uralistic tenden-
cies. For him, the
study of nature
was art's sole aim
and he rejected
any suggestion of
idealism or of ro-
manticism in his
approach. In this
respect, his pic-
tures express a
sober fidelity to
nature, the clear,
radiant brilliance
of which reminds
us of Kobell and
may be compared
with the early
work of Corot.

Of the Biedermeier painters, Friedrich von Amerling created a particularly brilliant form of society
portrait, for which—in addition to the Viennese tradition—his apprenticeship with Thomas Lawrence in
London and Horace Vernet in Paris gave him good grounding. One of his chief works, the family scene
illustrated on the facing page, gives us a typical example of the artist's noble style of painting. With the
clarity of a still life, it has an elegance which elsewhere can sometimes degenerate into an empty formula.

74

CHRISTEN KØBKE (1810–1848). *Frederiksborg Castle at Sunset.* 1835. Oil on canvas, 27¹/₈ × 39³/₄″. Den Hirschsprungske Samling, Copenhagen

In Danish painting, the Biedermeier period followed directly on from the Neoclassical without any Romantic interlude and, therefore, in the first half of the nineteenth century reached a purity as nowhere else. Kristoffer Vilhelm Eckersberg studied in Paris under David and afterward went to Rome. His pupil Christen Købke developed the work of the Danish Biedermeier school along its own individual lines and attained through the artistic freedom and brightness of his renderings a luminous facility and lightness reminiscent of the early Corot.

◀ KRISTOFFER VILHELM ECKERSBERG (1783–1853). *Morning Toilette.* 1837. Oil on canvas, 12¹/₄ × 9⁷/₈″. Den Hirschsprungske Samling, Copenhagen

KRÜGER. *Parade in Potsdam* (study for a painting of the same name in the former Winter Palace of St. Petersburg). 1849. Oil on paper on pasteboard, 14 × 21⁵/₈″. Kunsthalle, Bremen

Franz Krüger painted for the courts of Berlin and St. Petersburg. As a portraitist, as a painter of official ceremonies, and as an animal painter in the Berlin Biedermeier tradition, he has affinities with the landscape painter Johann Erdmann Hummel. Much in the cool clarity of his paintings connects him with Kobell. Krüger lacks a feeling for breadth of landscape and the detail of near objects predominates in his work. His painting conveys much of the Prussian and Berlin atmosphere and its cool serenity permeates his numerous official works, which stand in basic contradiction to the spirit of Biedermeier.

◀ FRANZ KRÜGER (1797–1857). *Prince Wilhelm out Riding, Accompanied by the Artist.* 1836. Oil on canvas, 12¹/₄ × 9¹/₂″. National-galerie, Berlin

Together with Christian Morgenstern, Georg von Dillis was the founder of the Munich landscape school. In his sketchlike paintings, the *bravura* of his artistic simplification—an element that will become increasingly important in the course of the nineteenth century right up to the time of the Impressionists—is developed in many complex ways into a new artistic principle. His works, the result of direct observation of nature, are among the finest examples of early landscape painting. In contrast to Waldmüller's objective naturalism, Dillis's view of everyday life is illuminated by his poetic conception of nature.

GEORG VON DILLIS (1759–1841). *Landscape with Ducal Mansion and Home Park*. c. 1800. Oil on paper on pasteboard, $7^5/_8 \times 10''$. Kunsthalle, Bremen

CARL ROTTMANN (1797–1850). *Wertheim am Main.* c. 1840. Oil on canvas, $12^5/_8 \times 18^3/_4''$. Kunsthalle, Hamburg

In the circle of Biedermeier painters, Romantic features began to emerge, most clearly in the work of Carl Rottmann. The early work illustrated here still lacks to a large extent the pretentious drama of his later paintings with their sense of "elegant" Romanticism.

KARL EDUARD FERDINAND BLECHEN (1798–1840). *The Neustadt-Eberswalde Rolling Mill.* c. 1834. Oil on wood, 10 × 12⁵/₈″. Staatliche Museen, Berlin

Karl Eduard Ferdinand Blechen's first trip to Italy took him from Romanticism to realism. His landscape studies were produced shortly after Corot's first visit to Italy, and their purely artistic outlook stands comparison with Corot's work. In contrast to Corot's springlike mood, however, Blechen places his color values in the dazzling light of summer. This art, in addition to that of Corot and Constable, represents a third development in large-scale landscape painting, in which color has become a means to make reality visual.

In spite of the realistic rendering, some element of Romanticism is also present. An interesting example of this is the picture of the rolling mill, which introduces into painting an industrial theme that had not previously been thought worthy of consideration. At the same time, Blechen transforms the mill into a romantically transfigured object which is no longer really in contrast with the contemplative idyll of the fishermen in the foreground. Nevertheless, this representation of a factory indicates possibilities which later on—especially in the work of Menzel—come to be depicted with greater directness.

BLECHEN. *Girls Bathing in the Terni Park.* 1828–29. Oil on canvas, 12³/₄ × 9³/₄″. Kunstmuseum, Düsseldorf ▶

Like Blechen's art, that of Louis Ferdinand von Rayski is determined by an openness of artistic form. His later works especially are quite free from the confines of the Biedermeier, from which they originated. In this connection, his stay in Paris in the years 1843–45 was important. There the painter was influenced particularly by Gros, Delacroix, Delaroche, and, above all, Géricault. With their uninhibited use of color, his portraits of noblemen have some affinity with those of Krüger.

Johan Christian Clausen Dahl developed landscape painting along the lines laid down by Friedrich and Carus and in the direction of the early realists. His pupil Christian Friedrich Gille continued along the same path, but with greater emphasis on the purely painterly tendencies of Dahl's works.

CHRISTIAN FRIEDRICH GILLE (1805–1899). *View of Dresden*. Oil on pasteboard, 9³/₄ × 12¹/₄″. Kunsthalle, Bremen

MORITZ VON SCHWIND (1804–1871). *The Morning Hour*.
1858. Oil on wood, 13³/₈ × 15³/₄″. Schackgalerie, Munich

The artistic inventiveness of Moritz von Schwind is supported by his marked talent for graphic description which belongs to the age of Romantic Biedermeier. The bright, sunlit, optimistic atmosphere in the room of *The Morning Hour* denotes a distinct departure from the secretively oppressive calm expressed by the early German Romantics—particularly by Kersting. This picture shows the undeniable talent of Schwind, who went astray and squandered his abilities by attempting monumental murals in the style of Peter von Cornelius—as, for example, the Wartburg frescoes.

Adrian Ludwig Richter's world is that of peasants, shepherds, and the petit-bourgeois idyll raised to a level of contemplativeness far removed from the happenings of the wider world. With art of this sort (which ran the risk of degenerating into insipidness) the artist had great success, especially with his innumerable illustrations for fairy-tales, legends, and tracts. The Neoclassical and the Romantic, especially that arising from the Nazarene tradition, come together in a unique way in Richter's art, which—in spite of its comparative limitations—gives form to a particular style of pious simplicity.

ADRIAN LUDWIG RICHTER (1803–1884). *Spring Evening (Evening Song)*. 1844. Oil on canvas, 28³/₈ × 42⁷/₈″. Kunstmuseum, Düsseldorf

CARL SPITZWEG (1808–1885). *The Sleeping Watchman*. c. 1875. Oil on cardboard, 11³/₈ × 7¹/₄″. Kurpfälzisches Museum, Heidelberg ▶

WILHELM BUSCH (1832–1908). *Hay Harvest*. Late 1880s. Oil on paper on pasteboard, $8^{1}/_{2} \times 9^{3}/_{4}$". Wilhelm-Busch-Museum, Hanover

Wilhelm Busch, although he was chiefly known as a caricaturist, was influenced, like Carl Spitzweg, by the school of Munich. The old Dutch and Flemish painters, especially Frans Hals and Adriaen Brouwer, had had such a strong influence on him that, after a period of study spent in imitation of Netherlandish art, he continued to paint intimate scenes independently. His late landscapes especially attain a surprising level of freedom in their sketchlike form and painterly execution. If they are compared with contemporary works of the Impressionists in France, it becomes obvious that they have nothing in common; the Impressionist art was based on open-air studies, but Busch's work originated in the quite different Baroque tradition.

Within the group of Biedermeier Romantics, Carl Spitzweg is a distinctive painter whose outstanding talent was dissipated in trivial anecdote and humorous idylls of small-town life. The experiences which the Munich painter had gained on his travels to Paris, Belgium, and London with the Barbizon painters, Diaz de la Peña and Delacroix, are lost in his small-scale works, which, despite all his artistic mastery, show an ever-present threat of mediocrity.

"Painting consists solely in the representation of objects which the artist can see and touch. ... I am firmly of the opinion that painting is first and foremost a concrete art and can only consist in the representation of real objects of everyday life. ... It speaks a completely physical language," declared Gustave Courbet. He aspired to programmatic realism in his art and tried to give it a social function. When his work was rejected by the committee of the International Exposition of 1855, in protest he set up his *Pavillon du Réalisme* as a counterdemonstration and manifesto, and exhibited in it forty of his own paintings.

Courbet's work, unencumbered by any doctrinal message, had a revolutionary effect. The very subjects chosen—for example, a pair of real-life wrestlers instead of Hercules and Antaeus, a scene of the everyday world instead of a legend—set new goals for painting. Courbet turned away from all traditional themes. In that sense and with his correspondingly heavy, violent use of color, he became, together with Delacroix, one of the principal forerunners of Impressionism. His pictures were powerfully constructed in broad, thickly applied sweeps of color, and gave reality the form of a robust and serious still life. Courbet envisaged his paintings as an expression of the revolutionary ideas of his friend Pierre-Joseph Proudhon, the socialist. He visited Germany several times, where he had a great influence on Hans Thoma, Wilhelm Leibl, and others.

JEAN-DÉSIRÉ-GUSTAVE COURBET (1819–1877). *Wrestlers*. 1853. Oil on canvas, 99¼ × 78". Museum of Fine Arts, Budapest

COURBET. *La Roche de dix heures* (near Ornans). 1855. Oil on canvas, $33^3/_4 \times 63''$. The Louvre, Paris

About *The Painter's Studio,* which was among the pictures shown at the protest exhibition of 1855, Courbet wrote: "I am in the center, painting; on the right are all those who have some part in the work, i.e., friends, colleagues, and artlovers. On the left, on the other hand, is the other world, the life of every day, the people, misery, wealth, poverty, exploiters and exploited, people who make a living out of death. ..." In this outstanding work, the masterly manner of the painting and the sweep of the composition overshadow the difficulties of the complex theme of the *"allégorie réelle,"* an interesting picture to set against the crowning achievement of Ingres.

COURBET. *The Painter's Studio.* 1855. Oil on ▶ canvas, $11'10'' \times 19'7^1/_2''$. The Louvre, Paris

DAUMIER. *The Dream of the Inventor of the Needle Gun.* 1866. Lithograph, 9$\frac{1}{4}$ × 7$\frac{3}{4}$". Kunsthalle, Bremen

Honoré Daumier, who was known primarily as a graphic artist, began his career as a political caricaturist. Although he was held in great esteem by his contemporaries, he did not become known as a painter until late in life. A satirical bent and a love of realism were mingled with Romantic features in his magnificent artistic production. Aloof from the demands of officially commissioned works with their representational or heroic style, his art recognizes the tragedy of human life and has great sensitivity. His religious pictures are unusual. The Essen painting (facing page) has definite connections with the work of Rembrandt and in its silhouette-like treatment of the figures, its use of light and shade, and the dramatic development of the scene by purely artistic means, it illustrates the main qualities of this great painter's style. *The Dream of the Inventor of the Needle Gun* affords a good example of the satirical acuity of Daumier the moralist. The confrontation of a single figure with a crowd merging into a threatening unity is a frequent theme with this artist. In this respect, the lithograph has much in common with the *Ecce Homo.*

PAUL-GUSTAVE DORÉ (1832–1883). *Ship Among Icebergs*. 1876. Gouache, 23¼ × 18″. Cabinet des Estampes, Musée de la Ville, Strasbourg

VICTOR-MARIE HUGO (1802–1885). *Non liber monet, non gladius servat* (or *Saint Paul*). 1850. India ink, charcoal, and watercolor, 24⅜ × 18½″. Maison de Victor Hugo, Paris

Gustave Doré was the most productive and successful book illustrator of the second half of the nineteenth century. Illustrations for the works of Dante, Cervantes, and Balzac are among his main works, in which Romantic tradition is often intensified into the macabre. In this way, Doré achieved a freedom of artistic technique which has enjoyed a revival of popularity in our own century.

Victor Hugo's graphic works correspond to the Romantic visions of his poetry; they have a fascinating quality that is carried along by an impulsive expressivity peculiar to Hugo. Emotional values, even the chance outlines of an unintentional ink spot, are all put to use. Hugo's artistic works and their connections with Romanticism are significant as potent, and at the same time intimate, accompaniments to his poetic oeuvre.

PAUL-GAVARNI (1804–1866). *The Muse of Painting*. 1839. Lithograph

Constantin Guys started out as a military cartoonist and, in the course of his development, his own innate talent for the telling picture evolved into a characteristic color drawing which attacked not only established customs but also the general character of a certain contemporary social class. He acquired distinction as a chronicler, in the widest sense, of the Second Empire, and was a draftsman and watercolorist of exceptional talent. His watercolors transpose observations of society into arresting artistic form free of any need for commentary; their modern emphasis was especially important for Manet's development.

Paul Gavarni worked, as Daumier did, for illustrated periodicals of the time. His drawings, full of meaning and accurate observation, depict the life of contemporary society in Paris, the world of the petits bourgeois and the artists. In contrast to Daumier's more penetrating observations, Gavarni used his talent for amiable frivolity to show up life's more amusing aspects.

CONSTANTIN GUYS (1802–1892). *Seated Dancer in a Crinoline*. Watercolor and brush over pencil sketch, 10¹/₄ × 7″. Kunsthalle, Bremen

The English painter and poet William Blake was a powerful force in esoteric Romanticism in the nineteenth century. His mystical conception of the world (which met with no understanding until the Pre-Raphaelite generation of mid-century) developed its own cosmogony and mythology, with the Bible and its Jewish commentators, Swedenborg, Böhme, Milton, and Plotinus as its sources. Blake's art anticipated the essential forms of Art Nouveau.

Blake's contemporary, John Henry Fuseli, was sixteen years older. His art originated in the *Sturm und Drang* period and developed as a special form of Romantically mannered painting. His most important works were based on literary themes and he was particularly influenced in matters of form by Michelangelo. Fuseli, who was also active as a writer, published his *Lectures on Painting* between 1801 and 1820.

JOHN EVERETT MILLAIS (1829–1896). *Ophelia*. 1852.
Oil on canvas, 30 × 44". Tate Gallery, London

John Everett Millais founded the "Pre-Raphaelite Brotherhood" together with Dante Gabriel Rossetti and William Holman Hunt in 1848. The program that they formulated rejected the classical and academic tradition, and in its place these artists demanded an accurate observation of nature; Millais especially strove after realism. At the same time, Rossetti, in particular, stood for a Romantic approach, which had a direct connection with the Nazarenes. Blake was important to the Pre-Raphaelites, whose understanding of Botticelli and the painting of the Quattrocento (before Raphael) was based on its emotional content rather than on its formal values. They are contemporaries of the German-Romans Böcklin and Feuerbach. Their tendency toward Romanticism became more and more pronounced in the course of time and influenced later artists such as William Morris and Edward Burne-Jones.

Adolph Friedrich Erdmann von Menzel produced an unusual form of historical picture in which he attempted to depict the past as present-day reality. He tried to carry this out in the most objective way possible, with the result that those works lack any element of idealistic pathos. Along with scenes from Prussian history and from court life there is this representation of an iron mill, depicting the world of the worker —without any of Blechen's Romantic transfiguration, but also without any socialist pathos.

ADOLPH FRIEDRICH ERDMANN VON MENZEL (1815–1905). *Iron Mill.* 1875. Oil on canvas, $60^1/_4 \times 99^5/_8$″. Nationalgalerie, Berlin

MENZEL. *Lighted Stairwell at Night*. 1848. Oil on pasteboard, 14⅝ × 8⅝". Folkwang Museum, Essen

MENZEL. *The Arist's Sister with Candle*. 1847. Oil on canvas, 18⅛ × 12⅝". Bayerische Staatsgemäldesammlungen, Munich

Menzel combines in his own special way a pronounced sense of realism with a great wealth of sensitivity. His early work has connections with the Berlin Biedermeier group, especially with Franz Krüger, but Menzel soon developed the early impressionistic approach which became so characteristic for him. This style of unfettered painting followed the tradition of nineteenth-century pleinairism and carried over the qualities of a sketch into the finished work. In this sense his art can be compared with the products of Constable's genius. The paintings from the period between 1845 and 1855 are important evidence for Menzel's fine artistic qualities, for his special sense for the unusual as a permanent record of something prosaic yet emotionally charged, and for his descriptive ability which extends far beyond the scene represented. The ill-lit staircase (facing page) not only gives the feeling of a Berlin lodging house but also contrives to convey the atmosphere of 1848, the year of revolution.

The way in which Menzel could exploit the possibilities of realism, and through his objectivity could illuminate specific objects and the mood they engender, is shown in the charming picture of his sister in the doorway (above). One can still perceive here some late effects of Biedermeier clarity, the limits of which are, however, extended. A comparison with Ferdinand Georg Waldmüller's village scenes, which sometimes slip into sentimentality, establishes this clearly. Menzel's own attitude to his early "Impressionist" years was curious. Later on he rejected Impressionism as sheer laziness, although even his late work still showed important possibilities in this direction.

CARL SCHUCH (1846–1903). *By the Wesslinger See*. 1876.
Oil on canvas, 17¹/₂ × 27⁵/₈″. Kunsthalle, Bremen

WILHELM LEIBL (1844–1900). *Three Women in Church*.
1882. Oil on canvas, 44¹/₂ × 30¹/₄″. Kunsthalle, Hamburg

The Viennese painter Carl Schuch—one of the most talented artists in the Leibl group—concentrated his abilities on the purely picturesque in the manner of Leibl, and developed them to an amazing extent. The shimmering color of this landscape is characteristic of his art and of the meaning he gave to his coloring, concerning which he wrote: "The significance of color shading is that it subtracts from objects their material quality and retains only the aesthetic essence of the scene."

After Wilhelm Leibl's art had already assumed a form of its own, he went, on Courbet's advice, to Paris. The *Three Women in Church*—his most famous painting—attained a peak never to be surpassed. It originated in Bavaria, in Leibl's so-called "Holbein period," in which his accurate eye for realistic detail produced something of a photographic effect, picking out details as though seen from close-to. At the same time, the picture's large format and sense of calm are also eloquent, balancing the effect of the clear, strong colors. Ingres's ideal of a synthesis between form and color emerges once more in completely different artistic conditions.

Leibl's painting strongly influenced German art of his time. None of those, however, who were inspired by him possessed his modest simplicity of mind or artistic intensity. Wilhelm Trübner's art is much more intellectual and has less force. Besides Courbet, who influenced all the painters in the Leibl group, the portrait reproduced above reminds us of that French intellectual tradition which Manet was to raise to the heights of genius.

The art of Hans Thoma has ambiguities and in its later phase unfortunately often sinks below the level of its earlier achievements. *The Falls of the Rhine at Schaffhausen* shows in a still intact form Thoma's ability to bring out in a realistic way the specific qualities of a certain landscape as peculiar to his homeland. Here again, this artist cannot be considered without mentioning Courbet—in 1868 Thoma had visited Paris with Otto Scholderer—and he produced his finest work in the seventies after joining up with Leibl and his friends in Munich.

WILHELM TRÜBNER (1851–1917). *Lady in Gray*. 1876. Oil on canvas, 41³/₄ × 36⁵/₈″. Folkwang Museum, Essen

HANS THOMA (1839–1924). *The Falls of the Rhine at Schaffhausen*. 1876. Oil on canvas, 33¹/₈ × 44⁷/₈″. Kunsthalle, Bremen

CARL FREDRIK HILL (1849–1911). *Seine Landscape.* 1877. Oil on canvas, $19^5/_8 \times 23^5/_8$″. Nationalmuseum, Stockholm

Carl Fredrik Hill is Sweden's most important landscape artist of this period. His exceptional talent was developed, under the influence of the French masters, into an individual style. Up to 1878, he was active as a landscape painter in France, where Corot, the Barbizon school, and Courbet had an influence on him. From Corot came the inspiration for Hill's realistic plein-air painting which led in his last years in Paris to Impressionism. The sketches in color which were produced after his Parisian period are not widely known. Their schizophrenic expression has a shock effect which suggests Expressionistic possibilities.

Ernst Josephson's art constitutes, after that of Hill, Sweden's second important contribution to the art of the nineteenth century. Together with the masterly sense of realism in his portraits, there is to be found in his work symbolism tinged with irony. From this two-sided talent there resulted works of great distinction. In 1888, Josephson suffered a mental illness and afterward created work in which the pathological and the artistic are intermingled.

Ernst Josephson (1851–1906). *Jeanette Rubenson*. 1883. Oil on wood, $16^{1}/_{8} \times 12^{3}/_{4}''$. Konstmuseum, Göteborg

MATTHIJS MARIS (1839–1917). *Souvenir of Amsterdam.* 1871. Oil on canvas, 18¼ × 13¾". Rijksmuseum, Amsterdam

JOZEF ISRAELS (1824–1911). *We Grow Old.* 1878. Oil on canvas, 63 × 39¾". Haags Gemeentemuseum, The Hague

Jozef Israels's painting stems from the discoveries of the realists and from the anecdotal approach, often sentimental, that was typical of the Düsseldorf school. Novotny quotes as a characteristic of this art Israels's own statement that, except for Millet, there was no painter who knew so little about painting and drawing as he did, but at the same time produced such good pictures.

Matthijs was the second of the three Maris painter-brothers, who belonged to the "Hague school." The landscape work of this group has affinities with the Barbizon school. In addition, there was the influence of the great tradition of landscape painting in Holland of the seventeenth century.

PÁL SZÍNYEI-MERSE (1845–1920). *The Picnic in May*. 1873. Oil on canvas, 48³/₈ × 63¹/₂". Museum of Fine Arts, Budapest

The Hungarian painter Pál Színyei-Merse came into close contact with the Leibl circle in Munich and was there strongly influenced by them. His most famous picture, *The Picnic in May,* is noteworthy for its enhanced color values, an inheritance from Courbet and the French Impressionists translated into a specifically Hungarian setting.

In Anton Romako's finest pictures, the artistic stimulus of which transforms the then fashionable interest in anecdote into psychological insight, Novotny sees precursors of Kokoschka's early Expressionist portraits. The painting of the Battle of Lissa (facing page) shows how Romako strove to produce the most direct representation possible of a moment of supreme danger, and in so doing added a new dimension to the sphere of battle painting.

ANTON ROMAKO (1832–1889). *Admiral Tegetthoff at the Battle of Lissa.* 1878. Oil on wood, 43¹/₄ × 32¹/₄". Österreichische Galerie, Vienna ▶

Ilya Efimovich Repin (1844–1930). *The Cossacks Drafting a Letter to the Sultan.* 1880–91. Oil on canvas, 7′ 1½″ × 11′ 10″. Russian Museum, Leningrad

Ilya Efimovich Repin is the best-known representative of naturalism in Russian art of the nineteenth century, and shows pronounced social tendencies as a convinced supporter of the "Peredvishniki" group. In addition to portraits, he painted genre and historical pictures from Russia's folklore and history. His painting has a special significance for the development of Russian art, and brought with it the impressions that Repin had collected from his apprenticeship in Paris. It acted as a focus for the forces of the new art in Russia at the turn of the century.

ANSELM FEUERBACH (1829–1880). *The Banquet of Plato*. 1873.
Oil on canvas, 13′ 1¹/₂″ × 24′ 7″. Nationalgalerie, Berlin

In the second half of the nineteenth century, together with efforts toward realism, an intellectual style of painting was also evolved in which—along with the English Pre-Raphaelites—the so-called German-Romans played an important part. Feuerbach and Böcklin are the chief representatives of this movement.

For Anselm Feuerbach it was a question of portraying a noble world of aristocratic beings, structured in a coolly classical way and displaying a delicate and eloquent use of color. As well as by the Düsseldorf school, Feuerbach was influenced by Thomas Couture and above all (he traveled to Italy in 1855) by the Venetian painters, especially Titian and Veronese. He never completely avoided the danger, inherent in his ultraclassical approach, of losing himself in pure aestheticism.

Puvis de Chavannes can be placed alongside the Pre-Raphaelites and the German-Romans as the most significant French representative of an idealistic and intellectual type of painting. His particular feeling for the value of the surface and of its constituent parts destined him for mural painting, and it is in this that he achieved renown. In his work, a calm, sometimes rather pallid and academic, world is portrayed, lacking the taut pretensions of Feuerbach. It is, however, precisely in this strange, colorless neutrality that the special effect of his art resides.

PIERRE-CÉCILE PUVIS DE CHAVANNES (1824–1898). *Beside the Sea.* 1879. Oil on canvas, 24 × 18½″. The Louvre, Paris

The Swiss painter Arnold Böcklin spent much of his artistic life in Germany. There he became more popular than Menzel, which J. Meier-Graefe explained as being due to "the eruption of current folk art which Richard Wagner had brought into being. [Böcklin] has this in common with Feuerbach, that he failed to recognize his own innate capacities and consequently slipped over onto a downward path."

ARNOLD BÖCKLIN (1827–1901). *The Sacred Grove*. 1886. Oil on wood, 39³/₈ × 59″. Kunstmuseum, Basel

BÖCKLIN. *Odysseus and Calypso*. 1883. Tempera on mahogany, 41 × 59″. Kunstmuseum, Basel

For Böcklin as for others, Italy, where he also spent much of his life, afforded fundamental artistic impressions. Many of his best paintings were produced there. His art develops into a picture with symbolical and literary meaning, which can only partially be understood by reference to purely artistic standards. Because of this, his use of color becomes more and more sharply contrasted and defies the laws of chromatic harmony which he had initially composed and observed. Böcklin's pictures have a strange fractured quality about them—his contrived themes acquire the directness of a genre painting—and have something in common with the Surrealist developments of the twentieth century.

HANS VON MARÉES (1837–1887). *Diana Bathing*. 1863. Oil on canvas, $37^3/_8 \times 52^3/_4''$. Bayerische Staatsgemäldesammlungen, Munich

Although Hans von Marées is also defined as a German-Roman, his connection with Feuerbach and Böcklin is a very superficial one. The basic theme of his work is the human figure in a landscape, and his pictures exclude all concern for realistic portrayal. He endeavors to realize ideas by means of form without going to the trouble of relating stories, myths, or legends in order to do so. The large-scale, dynamic nature of his paintings led him inevitably toward murals. More expressive than Ingres, Marées, the second great Neoclassicist of the nineteenth century, was a distinguished painter in whose work color is the element that holds the picture together and invests it with a many-sided mystery.

MARÉES. *Evening Forest Scene*. c. 1870. Oil on canvas, $24^3/_4 \times 20^1/_8''$. Kunsthalle, Bremen

GUSTAVE MOREAU (1826–1898). *Jupiter and Semele.* 1896. Oil on canvas, 84 × 40¹/₂″. Musée Gustave Moreau, Paris

ODILON REDON (1840–1916). *The Cyclops.* 1895–1900. Oil on wood, 25¹/₄ × 20″. Rijksmuseum Kröller-Müller, Otterlo

Along with Puvis de Chavannes, Gustave Moreau can also be named as a painter in whose work intellectual considerations predominate. He conceived his heterogeneous work, with its symbolism and mysticism, as an alternative to realism. Odilon Redon is related to Moreau in this respect. Redon's dream visions, which he began to create in the 1870s, are entirely based on symbolical ideas.

JAMES ENSOR (1860–1949). *The Entry of Christ into Brussels*. 1888. Oil on canvas, 8′ 6″ × 14′ 2″. On loan to Koninklijk Museum voor Schone Kunsten, Antwerp. Facing page: detail

James Ensor, who ranks today as the most famous of the modern Belgian painters, produced his best work between the years 1879–98, but it did not receive proper recognition and evaluation until after 1900. Having previously been rejected by the critics, its Fauvist, Expressionist, and Surrealist features were retrospectively recognized after the turn of the century, although Ensor can really hardly be considered as a forerunner of these movements. Ensor started out with interior studies painted in the Impressionist manner, in which he nevertheless showed the special expressivity of his use of color. After 1883, the range of his palette becomes bright and powerful. At the same time, new themes make their appearance and become typical of his work: skeletons, masks, Biblical subjects, in which heightened expression is exaggerated into something verging on the sardonic. These paintings are oppressive, but this gives them at the same time a distinctly naive effect. Their demand on the emotional response is strong, and the problem of form is often submerged in heterogeneous complexity.

IGNACE-HENRI-JEAN-THÉODORE FANTIN-LATOUR (1836–1904). *Flowers and Fruit*. 1865. Oil on canvas, 25¼ × 22½″. The Louvre, Paris

Fantin-Latour and Jongkind precede the great turning point of Impressionism with which the realistic tradition in nineteenth-century painting reaches its highest achievement. Fantin-Latour's painting combines the technique of "intellectual art"—he was one of the French admirers of Wagner—with the artistic resources of Courbet, all bathed in the superficially romantic melancholy of subdued lighting.

Johan Barthold Jongkind's pictures not only set free the art of his native Holland from its pastoral seclusion, but also paved the way for the light techniques of the Impressionists. Only the early part of his career was spent in Holland, and it was not until he reached Paris that his impressionistic development began. "To him I owe the final perfecting of my art," said Monet of Jongkind, whom he met in 1862, together with Boudin, at Le Havre.

JOHAN BARTHOLD JONGKIND (1819–1891). *The Harbor of Rotterdam.* 1856. Oil on canvas, $22^1/_2 \times 27^1/_8$". Stedelijk Museum, Amsterdam

Louis-Eugène Boudin's art was influenced above all by Corot and Jongkind, and his use of subtle nuance in color when portraying light prepared the way for the Impressionists. He was the teacher of Claude Monet, who received vital inspiration from him.

LOUIS-EUGÈNE BOUDIN (1824–1898). *The Jetty at Deauville.* 1869. Oil on wood, 9 × 12⁵/₈″. The Louvre, Paris

ÉDOUARD MANET (1832–1883). *Le Déjeuner sur l'herbe*. 1863. Oil on canvas, 84 × 106″. The Louvre, Paris

MANET. *The Game of Croquet*. 1873. Oil on canvas, 28¹/₂ × 41³/₄″. Städelsches Kunstinstitut, Frankfurt am Main

Edouard Manet, like Feuerbach, was a student of Couture, but his painting is in complete contrast to that of Feuerbach. Both sought inspiration from the Old Masters, but for the Frenchman these served primarily as a springboard for the development of his own principles. *Le Déjeuner sur l'herbe* (page 131) draws on works by Raphael and Giorgione, and yet reacts against them. Even this early work shows the undeniable vigor of Manet's painting: the entire subject matter seems presented on one single plane as brilliant foreground painting, unencumbered by any intellectual profundities. Manet's work influenced the palette and characteristic brushwork of Impressionism. He in his turn was very much affected by Impressionist plein-air painting, especially in the 1870s. Thus, he played his part in the movement by both influencing it and being influenced by it; but at the same time, he towered above it. He is more concerned with a firmly structured composition than with the shimmering, dreamlike, open-space atmosphere of Impressionism. Here his masterly handling of planes again becomes noticeable, especially in his later works. His main theme is the human figure, which in juxtaposition to the other objects in the picture appears remarkably like a still life.

MANET. *At Père Lathuille's*. 1879. Oil on canvas, 36⅝ × 44⅛". Musée des Beaux-Arts, Tournai

MANET. *A Bar at the Folies-Bergère*. 1881–82. Oil on canvas, 37¹/₂ × 51″. Courtauld Institute Galleries, London

The importance of Manet's work and of that of his contemporaries and followers lay in the interest shown in spatial organization. This development led to the discovery of the two-dimensional style of Oriental art, which in turn provided stimulating new ideas. Whistler's painting (below) is a typical example of this style and of the fashion for Oriental objects in general.

JAMES ABBOTT MCNEILL WHISTLER (1834–1903). *Caprice in Purple and Gold, No. 2: The Golden Screen.* 1864. Oil on wood, 19⅝ × 27″. Courtesy of the Smithsonian Institution, Freer Gallery of Art, Washington, D.C.

CLAUDE-OSCAR MONET (1840–1926). *Meadows in Springtime*.
1887. Oil on canvas, 29$^1/_4$ × 36$^5/_8$″. Staatsgalerie, Stuttgart

This type of picture by Claude Monet demonstrates how, in the illusory, vision-like canvases of Impressionism, color begins to be separated out into its individual elements; consequently the scene and the subject matter lose their importance and painting becomes an end in itself. The Impressionists showed less interest in detailed description than in the way an object appears, and this led to experiments with color forms and tones as autonomous pictorial values.

Monet's cathedral series, an example of which is shown here, pursues this problem in a sequence depicting the cathedral at different times of the day and in varying lights. The building as subject becomes largely unimportant, while the nuances of color and their actual appearance within the variations of the series become the real theme.

MONET. *Rouen Cathedral.* 1894. Oil on canvas, $42^1/_8 \times 28^3/_4''$. The Louvre, Paris

Claude Monet is the most influential exponent of French Impressionism. After the exhibition of 1874, his painting *Impression: Sunrise* gave its name to the whole movement—a name originally used as a term of derision.

Monet's painting shows the world as nothing but appearance reflected in light. As a result, the value of everyday things, of the momentary chance occasion, is discovered and found worthy of depiction. In this sense, his work is realistic, that is, not determined by ideas expressed in the picture. At the same time, it is illusory, since everything appears as background—not as a tangible foreground but as a fleeting impression. Accordingly, pigment is applied cursorily and in patches of color without reproducing details. Instead, as the technique becomes independent as a particular style of painting, it disowns the recognizable subject of the picture. The actual occasion becomes of less and less importance, while that of the atmosphere of illusion increases, as we have seen, for example, in Monet's variations on Rouen Cathedral (page 137), showing the building in changing lights.

Alfred Sisley is very closely associated with Monet. However, this landscape from the Hamburg Kunsthalle illustrates how the strong painterly structure of his canvases, with the direct appeal of the composition that results from it, sets them apart. In this way, Sisley's work occupies a distinctive place among the developments of Impressionism. Paint, applied in small dabs in a manner characteristic of Impressionism, produces separate planes which, when reconstituted as a whole, bring about the formation of form and line through color. The strips of field converge to where trees and bushes rise up as a dominating motif which gathers to itself the total energy produced by the movements of the many small parts.

ALFRED SISLEY (1839–1899). *The Cornfield.* 1873.
Oil on canvas, $19^7/_8 \times 28^3/_4$". Kunsthalle, Hamburg

CAMILLE PISSARRO (1830–1903). *March Sunlight.* 1875. Oil on canvas, 21⅝ × 36⅛″. Kunsthalle, Bremen

Camille Pissarro was another of the pioneers of Impressionist painting, although he was rarely an innovator. Though receptive to the most varied influences, his open-mindedness never harmed his own creative ability. His canvases are always outstandingly sensitive and are among the finest testimonies of Impressionism. Cézanne spoke of Pissarro's art as "modest and colossal" and as a constant inspiration.

PIERRE-AUGUSTE RENOIR (1841–1919). *Luncheon of the Boating Party.* 1881. Oil on canvas, 51 × 68″. The Phillips Collection, Washington, D.C.

Auguste Renoir's work was sustained by a great talent the vigor and profusion of which has sometimes led to its being mistakenly regarded as frivolous. After Manet, whose greatest achievements he never quite equaled, Renoir is the second great painter among the Impressionists whose work is devoted to the theme of the human figure. Renoir's people do not appear, like Manet's, detached and almost solitary, but are fully rounded, sensual figures, full of liveliness when combined together in groups. The unusual colorfulness of his canvases

shows how impressed he was by Delacroix's interpretation of the Baroque style of painting. From the 1880s on, the female nude set in a landscape became Renoir's main theme. It is in the personification of living abundance amidst the flowering profusion of nature that his work is at its most perfect. The form and modeling of the body, inspired by Italian examples and especially by Raphael, go beyond the boundaries of Impressionism—as does Renoir's work in general.

The boundaries of Impressionism, perhaps best exemplified by Monet's work, cannot quite contain the work of Degas either. Degas always refused to let himself be described as an Impressionist. Ingres was his main inspiration and draftsmanship his prime concern. Degas searched for a new law governing the form of the human figure and its relationship to the surrounding space. To do this, he, unlike the Neoclassicists, started

EDGAR-HILAIRE-GERMAIN DEGAS (1834–1917). *Ballet School.* c. 1879–80. Oil on canvas, 16¹/₂ × 19¹/₄″. W. A. Clark Collection, Corcoran Gallery of Art, Washington, D. C.

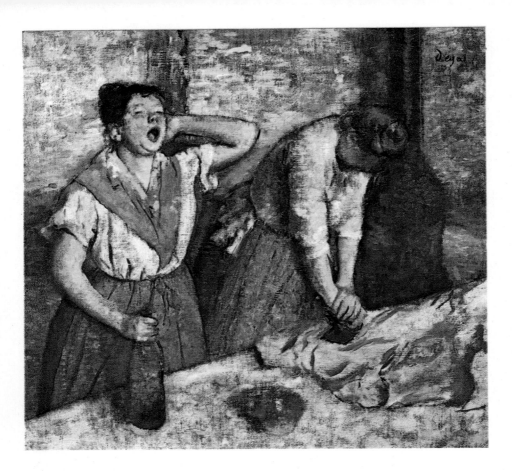

DEGAS. *Two Laundresses*. c. 1884. Oil on canvas, 30 × 32″. The Louvre, Paris

from very exact observation. In its treatment of the female body, his style reveals, as never before, its beauty as a colored form of unrivaled richness; yet there is no suggestion of eroticism. Degas's work never lacks an enchanting clarity, rejects all passionate involvement, and remains free from social criticism (cf. *Two Laundresses*), from the romance of the setting (cf. the ballet and cabaret pictures), and from literary profundities. Like Manet, Degas too was influenced by the flat spatial organization of Japanese woodcuts. His pictures are characterized by his treatment of the problem of fragmentation. Figures and objects are boldly cut into by the edge of the canvas. The resulting unresolved relationships between the different parts of the picture create tensions which are then caught up and resolved in the whole.

DEGAS. *Chanteuse au Gant (Café Singer Wearing a Glove)*. 1878. Pastel, 21 × 16¹/₄″. Fogg Art Museum, Harvard University, Cambridge, Mass. Maurice Wertheim Collection

PAUL CÉZANNE (1839–1906). *Mountains in Provence*. 1878–80. Oil on canvas, $21\frac{1}{4} \times 28\frac{3}{4}''$. Gwendoline Davis Bequest, National Museum of Wales, Cardiff

Although Paul Cézanne was associated with the Impressionists, his artistic path diverged from theirs. From the passionate dark scenes of his early figure paintings, inspired by examples of Baroque art which had been models for Delacroix's and Courbet's work, his canvases developed into well-balanced and many-sided creations. The landscape reproduced above shows Cézanne's characteristic method of applying the color in dabs—a technique derived from Impressionism. But the final effect differs from Impressionist painting in that the form and line of individual color values are more strictly organized into clearly defined planes. The whole picture is built up from a sequence of such planes: color and form depend on each other, one growing out of the other in mutual interdependence. This was a principle which Cézanne developed to a degree of perfection unrivaled by anyone else. Gradually, a structure built up of individual parts recalling stereometric forms becomes increasingly evident until it finally becomes axiomatic for this style of painting. Later, the Cubists were to regard this as a basic law.

Differing in this respect from the Impressionists, color in Cézanne's canvases does not turn into a free-floating web of brush strokes but exists in clearly defined areas. Cézanne commented: "There are no lines, no modeling, nothing but contrasts, and these are shown not by black-and-white but by the feeling of color." These canvases are based on "color-forms" (Kurt Badt) which combine in mutual dependence, entwined and bonded together to make a whole. To a far greater extent than was the case among his contemporaries and others, these basic elements of Cézanne's pictures are artistic formulations in line with the created reality of his canvases. This spells the end of the principle of "illusion." Cézanne spoke of art as "a harmony parallel to nature."

CÉZANNE. *Still Life with Apples and Oranges.* 1895–1900. Oil on canvas, $28^3/_4 \times 36^1/_4$". The Louvre, Paris

"To paint the true essence of an object, a painter needs eyes able to apprehend the object solely through color and, in combining it with other objects, to allow the motif to be created by color alone," said Cézanne. According to this, his color-form theory, he builds up his canvases from the interrelationship of solid areas of color. In *Bibémus Quarry,* one of his "Cubist" paintings, the massive stereometric cube shapes and the gradations of depth of the central area are closely bound to the surface of the picture. This surface, widely ignored by the Impressionists, is seen in an entirely new way and contains new possibilities for the treatment of space which no longer recognize the scientific laws of perspective.

CÉZANNE. *Bibémus Quarry.* 1898–1900. Oil on canvas, 25⁵/₈ × 31⁷/₈″. Folkwang Museum, Essen

CÉZANNE. *Bathers (Les Grandes Baigneuses).* 1898–1905. Oil on canvas, 82 × 98″. The Philadelphia Museum of Art. Wilstach Collection

GEORGES-PIERRE SEURAT (1859–1891). *A Sunday Afternoon on the Island of La Grande Jatte*. 1884–86.
Oil on canvas, 81 × 120″. The Art Institute of Chicago. Helen Birch Bartlett Memorial Collection

This painting by Georges Seurat provides a clear demonstration of the methods of Pointillism. The bright
colored palette of the Impressionists is rationalized, and this is done precisely in accordance with the scientific
discoveries of spectrum analysis. Color, no longer tied to the object, is applied in pointlike spots uniformly
distributed. Color, which in the pictorial relationships of Impressionist painting is used to describe the illusory charm of the surface, is now broken down into its constituent elements, approximately those of the
spectrum. It is then distributed according to its own law in such a way that the pictorial relationships become
apparent only when its synthesis takes place once more in the eye of the viewer. This style of painting, which
walks the tightrope between art and artifice, rationalizes the discoveries of the Impressionists. In competition

with Cézanne's formal and carefully constructed work, Pointillism (or Neo-Impressionism) indicates new ways of reorganizing the inheritance of Impressionism and of taking its place. Seurat and Signac were the chief exponents of this new movement, a movement which was to have an influence on the new generation of painters, especially on Van Gogh and his Expressionist followers.

PAUL SIGNAC (1863–1935). *Breakfast*. 1886–87. Oil on canvas, 35 × 45¼". Rijksmuseum Kröller-Müller, Otterlo

SIGNAC. *Advertisement for Charles Henry's "Cercle Chromatique"* in a program for André Antoine's Théâtre Libre. 1888. Color lithograph, $6^{1}/_{4} \times 7^{1}/_{8}$"

Paul Signac's close collaboration with Charles Henry underlines the connection between Pointillism and scientific thinking. The two publications for which Signac produced posters and advertisements are entitled "The Chromatic Circle, Containing All the Complementary Colors and Color Harmonies, with an Introduction to Dynamogeny or the Science of Contrasts, Rhythm, and Proportion," and "Aesthetic Tables with Instructions for Their Use in the Applied Arts, in the History of Art, in the Interpretation of Graphic Method and Generally for the Study and Aesthetic Improvement of Form." Signac, writing to Van Gogh says: "This is of real social importance, especially in the field of the applied arts. It enables us to teach workers and apprentices, whose aesthetic education until now consisted solely of empirical definitions and dishonest advice, how to see really beautifully."

Vincent Van Gogh, Dutch by birth, was obsessed from the very beginning with the need for an explicit statement of belief, a definite message to the brotherhood of Man. Because of this, he first started work as a lay
preacher. His somber early works are part social criticism. When Van Gogh went to Paris in 1886, Impressionism and Pointillism were the styles of the moment. Having tried out and assimilated the results of Impressionism, the Dutchman entered on a new phase. The palette of the Pointillists provided him with color

VINCENT WILLEM VAN GOGH (1853–1890). *The Loom*. 1884. Oil
on canvas, 27½ × 33½". Rijksmuseum Kröller-Müller, Otterlo

freed from local aspects. Van Gogh examined this material in the light of its intrinsic expressive value and then made use of it in his own works. Color as tone and as form then takes on an expressive function, especially in his later works. The fundamental atmosphere, neurotically clear-sighted, shatters the realistic representation of the visible world. The succeeding generation of twentieth-century Expressionists was greatly influenced by Van Gogh's discoveries.

VAN GOGH. *View of Montmartre.* 1886. Oil on canvas, 15¹⁄₈ × 24¹⁄₈". Öffentliche Kunstsammlung, Basel

VAN GOGH. *Road with Cypresses.* 1890. Oil on canvas, 36¹/₄ × 28³/₄″. Rijksmuseum Kröller-Müller, Otterlo

In 1886, Émile Bernard went on a journey to Normandy and Brittany, where he met Émile Schuffenecker and Paul Gauguin. In his posthumously published essay *On Symbolism*, Bernard writes: "In Brittany, where the Symbolist movement had its beginning, the landscape and the traditional hieratic elements are in harmony with the desires and aims of the Symbolists. Furthermore, there are a great number of churches, calvaries, and pilgrimages. This beloved country gave us what we sought and could find nowhere else—the *spectacles poétiques*."

ÉMILE BERNARD (1868–1941). *Breton Women in a Meadow*. 1886.
Watercolor and gouache, 17³/₄ × 20¹/₂". Kunsthalle, Bremen

PAUL GAUGUIN (1848–1903). *Breton Seaweed Gatherers.*
1889. Oil on canvas, 34¼ × 48″. Folkwang Museum, Essen

Gauguin's answer to the Neo-Impressionists' divisionism was a rearrangement of the canvas into flat areas. The pictorial principle used by him, and known as "cloisonnism" because of its similarities with that technique of enamelworking, dates back to Émile Bernard who, together with Louis Anquetin, first developed the new use of flat surfaces in the 1880s. Gauguin used Bernard's inventions in building up his own style as a parallel to Van Gogh's experiments. His vigorous flat areas of color exist as autonomous means of expression. From 1891 onward, Gauguin lived, apart from one break, on the South Sea islands of Tahiti and Dominica (Hiva Oa) in the Marquesas. His canvases show scenes from that world which, with their suggestion of the fantastic, appear like dream projects of a lost paradise.

IA ORANA MARIA

HENRI DE TOULOUSE-LAUTREC (1864–1901). *Poster for the Moulin Rouge*. 1891. Color lithograph, 67 × 51″. Musée Toulouse-Lautrec, Albi

Henri de Toulouse-Lautrec's work also diverged from Impressionism, while being stimulated by the style of Degas, Gauguin, and Japanese woodcuts. In the 1890s, he turned to lithography and enriched this technique in a variety of ways. In doing this, he turned the poster into an art form. He found his subjects in the demimonde—in the cafés, the cabarets, the circus, and on the racetrack—which makes his art significant as social criticism.

EDVARD MUNCH (1863–1944). *Puberty*. 1894. Oil on canvas, 59 × 43¹/₄″. Nasjonalgalleriet, Oslo

MUNCH. *The Cry.* 1895. Color lithograph, $13^3/_4 \times 10''$

Norway comes onto the scene of European art for the second time in the nineteenth century with the advent of Edvard Munch. This time it plays a more important part in the whole picture than it did at the time of Dahl and his contemporary, Thomas Fearnley. Munch lived in Paris from 1885 onward; he then went to Germany and did not return to Norway until 1909. His style, which depends on the expressive power of color and line, developed under the influence of Postimpressionism. The early Expressionist developments of this movement came to be accepted and emulated in Germany and the Nordic countries partly because of Munch. In his representation of human beings, Munch's aim, like that of August Strindberg in his writings, is to express fundamental emotions as directly as possible.

ÉDOUARD VUILLARD (1868–1940). *Mother and Child.* 1899. Oil on card-board on panel, 19 × 22¼". Glasgow Art Gallery and Museum

Édouard Vuillard and Pierre Bonnard belong among the Postimpressionists. Within the circle of the group of artists known as "Les Nabis" (the Prophets), they pursued an antinaturalistic art which led from Neo-Impressionist divisionism to a new, loosely knit surface composition. This development would have been unthinkable without Bernard's "cloisonnism" and Gauguin's energetic formulation of new surface organization. However, whereas with Gauguin this new art contains definite statements and messages—partly of a directly missionary character, and thus connected with Van Gogh's new pictures of the world—the work of Vuillard and Bonnard, from a thematic point of view, retains the freedom of the Impressionists. Interiors, street scenes, and similar insignificant subjects enable color to develop its poetic play in a loose arrangement of carpet-like flatness. This is important as a point of departure for the Fauves, whose unencumbered color depends only on its own glowing qualities. In contrast, the canvases of the Expressionists are heavily loaded with intellectual concepts.

PIERRE BONNARD (1867–1947). *Women and Children (The Grandmother)*. 1899. Oil on canvas, $21^5/_8 \times 22^1/_2''$. Musée National d'Art Moderne, Paris

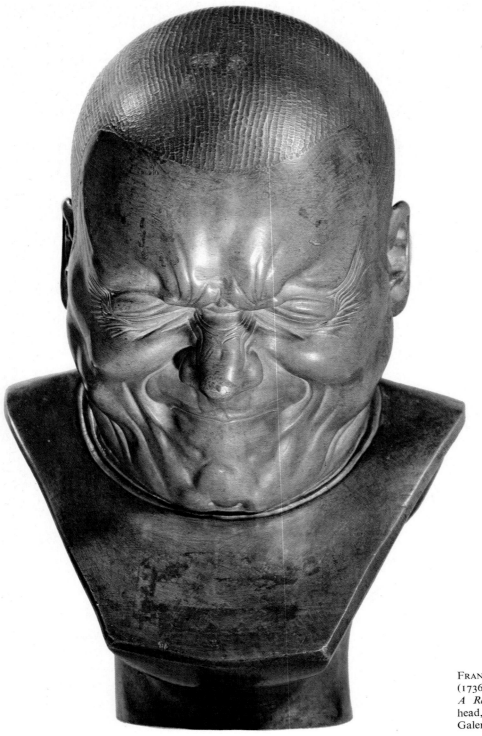

FRANZ XAVER MESSERSCHMIDT (1736–1783). *Character Head: A Rascal*. c. 1780. Height of head, 15³/₈″. Österreichische Galerie, Vienna

Franz Xaver Messerschmidt was one of the most important Late Baroque sculptors in Austria in the second half of the eighteenth century. The example shown opposite, one of his later works, belongs to a group of sculptures developed from a range of physiognomic studies made by him in the 1770s (similar to Johann Kaspar Lavater's *Physiognomic Studies*). The clear, simplified form of the sculptures which grew out of these studies reacts against their Baroque inheritance.

JEAN-ANTOINE HOUDON (1741–1828). *François-Marie-Arouet de Voltaire*. 1778. Marble, height 32¼″. Comédie-Française, Paris

The Frenchman Jean-Antoine Houdon, together with the Italian Canova, the German Schadow, the Swede Sergel, and the Dane Thorvaldsen, was a leading exponent of Neoclassical sculpture. Houdon's style has its beginnings in the Baroque, though later his Neoclassicism avoids doctrinaire "pure" sculpture. Instead, his work is distinguished by a special feeling for naturalness. This is most noticeable in his excellent portraits, which can stand comparison with the best of David's, though they show their Baroque inheritance more clearly than the latter's.

JOHN FLAXMAN (1755–1826). *The Apotheosis of Homer*. After 1780.
Wedgwood relief, $7^3/_4 \times 14^3/_4$". British Museum, London

This colored earthenware relief by the leading English exponent of Neoclassicism is a typical example of his
world based on Antique models. Flaxman's designs derive from the study of Greek vases and were executed
by Wedgwood.

K. Lankheit points out that the English Neoclassicist sculptors were decisively influenced by their recep-
tiveness to Gothic ideas as well as by their classical schooling. Flaxman's interest in the Gothic came about
through his friend William Blake.

The Alexander frieze was designed in 1812, in connection with the preparations for Napoleon's visit to Rome, as a surround for a banqueting hall in the Quirinal Palace. Through its subject—Alexander the Great entering Babylon—it alludes to Napoleon's visit. The balanced, finely modeled quality of relief carving, such as was used to realize this theme, was regarded by the artists of the time as the ideal artistic solution.

BERTEL THORVALDSEN (1768–1844). *Alexander the Great Entering Babylon* (detail). 1812. Plaster, height 46″, total length of frieze 86′ 10″. Quirinal Palace, Rome

Thorvaldsen, who shared his position as the best-known sculptor of his time with Canova, created his works under the influence of the great examples of Antiquity. Antiquity in Thorvaldsen's case meant Greek, not Roman, art. He himself collected Antique sculpture and in 1816 started to interest himself in the restoration of the recently discovered Aeginetan marbles. The untroubled repose of Greek statues is transformed in Thorvaldsen's figures into a romantic wish-fulfilling dreaminess.

ANTONIO CANOVA (1757–1822). *Napoleon I.* c. 1810. Marble, height to top of head 10′ 8″. Wellington Museum, London

In contrast to Houdon, Antonio Canova created figures belonging to a world of gods and heroes, and in them personified absolute values. The sitters portrayed by him appear an Antique guise, such as Pauline Borghese as Venus, George Washington as a Roman general, Napoleon as the colossal nude figure of an Imperator. Particularly in his female figures, Canova's art, in addition to its heroic side, can express a feeling of gentle nobility which, with its Rococo overtones, may degenerate into sickly sweetness. The portrait of Pauline Borghese has been compared with David's painting of Mme. Récamier—a comparison which demonstrates two distinct variations of Neoclassicism. Pierre-Paul Prud'hon was particularly attracted by Canova's work.

CANOVA. *Pauline Borghese as Venus.* 1807. Marble, life-size. Galleria Borghese, Rome

FRANÇOIS RUDE (1784–1855). *The Departure of the Volunteers in 1792 (La Marseillaise)* (detail). 1835–36. Stone relief, c. 42 × 26′
Arc de Triomphe, Paris

ERNST RIETSCHEL (1804-1861). *Monument to Goethe and Schiller*. 1857. Bronze. Weimar

The influences received by Rietschel from Rauch, who in turn was influenced by Schadow, in a student-teacher relationship help to retrace important developments in the nineteenth-century history of German sculpture. It starts with Rauch entrenched in Neoclassicism, which is then extended by Rietschel's efforts into a realism which finally displaces it.

Rude's main works are the reliefs on the Arc de Triomphe glorifying the French Revolution. This important example of Romantic sculpture is distinguished by the impetus that it conveys, the power of its moving masses, which has led to its being compared with Delacroix's *Liberty Leading the People*. Both works, though they differ in type and quality, react against the Baroque. The closest analogy is with Pierre Puget's violent style.

Unlike Canova and Thorvaldsen, Johann Gottfried Schadow's Neoclassicism does not exist in a theory-dominated world of heroes, gods, and titans. His lively sculpture starts in the Baroque tradition but leaves it almost completely for a style in which the values of Prussian middle-class sobriety are mixed with charm and gracefulness. In this context he can be compared to Daniel Nikolaus Chodowiecki. His greatest disciple was the North German sculptor Christian Daniel Rauch, who had been strongly influenced by Thorvaldsen in Rome, and whose sculptures, unlike those of Schadow, have a more immediate appeal. This may explain the innumerable commissions he received in his lifetime for portraits and monuments.

JOHANN GOTTFRIED SCHADOW (1764–1850). *Portrait Bust of Frau von Reibnitz*. 1800. Marble, height 23″. Kunsthalle, Bremen

CHRISTIAN DANIEL RAUCH (1777–1857). *Monument to Frederick the Great*. 1839–51. Bronze. Gardens of Sans-Souci, Potsdam

The two huge female figures of *Bavaria* and the *Statue of Liberty* belong to an important kind of monument typical of the nineteenth century. In this connection Johannes Schilling's Niederwald monument, erected in 1883, should also be mentioned. In addition to memorials of famous men, equestrian statues, and halls of fame such as Valhalla, these monuments were designed to express complex national and political ideals in anthropomorphic form.

LUDWIG VON SCHWANTHALER (1802–1848). *Bavaria*. 1837–48. Bronze, height c. 60′. Munich

FRÉDÉRIC-AUGUSTE BARTHOLDI (1834–1904). *Statue of Liberty*. 1871–84. Copper sheets mounted on steel frame (framework constructed by A.-G. Eiffel), height 152′. Liberty Island (Bedloe's Island), New York

Cologne Cathedral. West front.
Decoration of south door. 1842–80

These two examples show how widespread "interpretative" imitations were in nineteenth-century art. On the one hand, the artist in Cologne (facing page) turns toward Late Gothic forms already present in the cathedral, closely basing his style on them but developing it further. In spite of the nearness to the originals, the figures created by him seem much sharper in outline; the line cutting them off from the surrounding space stands out more strongly than the varied volumes of the figures themselves. This produces a certain stiffness which is also present in the Rococo-type decorations at Schloss Linderhof. Here, the similarity to the originals is astounding.

Sconce with putto in bedroom of Schloss Linderhof, Bavaria. c. 1870

Antoine-Louis Barye started as a painter, was taught by Gros, and was strongly influenced by Géricault and Delacroix. He produced almost nothing but animal sculptures and shared the Romantic preference for representing wild beasts fighting or preying on others. In this he modeled himself on Delacroix.

ANTOINE-LOUIS BARYE (1795–1875). *Jaguar Devouring a Hare*. 1851. Bronze, 16$^{1}/_{2}$ × 37$^{1}/_{2}$″. The Louvre, Paris

EMMANUEL FRÉMIET (1824–1910). *Orangutan Strangling a Native of Borneo.* 1895. Marble, height 76³/₄″. Musée d'Histoire Naturelle.
Jardin des Plantes, Paris

Emmanuel Frémiet's animal sculptures show the influence of his uncle, François Rude, especially in their striving after highly dramatic scenes. Their exotic themes belong to that group of subjects so dear to French Romanticism, and sometimes they fail to escape from the purely anecdotal.

DAUMIER. *Self-Portrait*. 1853. Bronze, height 28³/₈". Bibliothèque Nationale, Paris

DAUMIER. *Fugitives*. 1848–49. Bronze, 14⁵/₈ × 29⁷/₈″. Kunsthalle, Bremen

"The relief *Les Fugitifs* looks as if sketched by a Michelangelo who no longer felt in need of the Antique. These things may have affected the few contemporaries who saw them as much as Matisse's bronzes affected the peaceable citizens of our time. ... This sculpture has a thousand possibilities that were not available to the Old Masters. ... The method taken from painting which is first used in this relief brought sculpture face to face with the alternative either to deny entirely the direction of this development or to disappear" (J. Meier-Graefe).

After 1830, Daumier started modeling small busts initially as sketches for lithographs. Of his later sculptural works, the statue of *Ratapoil* and the relief illustrated above were the only two pieces known for a long time. Since then, others have reappeared, such as the powerful self-portrait on the facing page. Just as Daumier's lithographs are the product of their dynamic pictorial line and his portrait paintings are built up from the effects of separate brush strokes, so his sculpture is made to live by the painterly articulation of the surface, whose plastic value is reduced to an almost sketchy abbreviation.

CARPEAUX. *Dance.* 1866–69. Stone, height 10′ 10″. Facade of the Opéra, Paris

Jean-Baptiste Carpeaux was Rude's student, but in his sculptures invented a new form depending on a strongly agitated surface. His work combines Baroque traditions (especially Houdon) with painterly realism. Carpeaux translated the possibilities of painting into terms of sculpture, as is shown to its greatest effect in his group depicting *Dance.*

RENOIR. *Woman Suckling Her Child.* 1916. Bronze, height 21¼". Kunsthalle, Bremen

In his last years, the painter Auguste Renoir, crippled by arthritis, produced several sculptures with the help of an assistant. The work reproduced above is an almost exact copy of one of his paintings of 1885. In these sculptures, the Impressionist delight in the surface, which necessarily includes sculptural "handwriting" as artistic value, is combined with a very careful search for form. This is also evident in the paintings of this artist, often regarded as being lacking in attack.

In his lifetime Edgar Degas exhibited only one sculpture (the famous young ballet dancer in a tulle skirt, now in the Metropolitan Museum of Art, New York). All his other sculptures known to us came to light only after his death, at which time they were cast in bronze whenever that was still possible. They mostly consist of studies in movement, and in their search for new laws of form they pursue the same path as his drawings and paintings. The sculptures also show that they have something in common with Impressionism, but differ radically from it in their severe form based on classical models.

DEGAS. *Dancer at Rest*. Bronze, height 17³/₄".
Kunsthalle, Bremen

FRANÇOIS-AUGUSTE-RENÉ RODIN (1840–1917). *The Man with the Broken Nose*. 1864. Bronze, height 10¹⁄₈″. Kunsthalle, Bremen

Auguste Rodin looked mainly to the great examples of Michelangelo and of Gothic sculpture for his inspiration, while the fundamentals of his work are also present in Degas. Important influences can be traced to Carpeaux, as is plainly visible in one of his early works, *The Man with the Broken Nose*. Here, Carpeaux's experiments with a "painterly" sculpture are developed by Rodin who, through the deliberate use of forms which are sketched in and incomplete, produces a dramatic movement of the sculptural elements. Furthermore, there is a quality of suffering, vital in Rodin's work, which usually finds expression in his symbolical figures and groups, and which appears in greatest variety in the never completed *Gates of Hell* (facing page).

RODIN. *The Gates of Hell.*
Begun 1880. Bronze, height
c. 20′. Musée Rodin, Paris

RODIN. *The Burghers of Calais*. 1884–88. Bronze, height 83″. Kunstmuseum, Basel

Rodin's famous monument *The Burghers of Calais* is a narrative group of figures that transcends the boundaries of self-contained sculpture—more so even than Carpeaux's works. Thus, it both opens up the way to new developments and poses problems concerning the very nature of sculpture itself. *The Sculptor's Dream* (facing page) shows evidence of Rodin's preoccupation with Michelangelo. From him derives Rodin's treatment of the raw material, whose powerful function is brought out by the relationship between the figures comprised in the work and the total form of the sculpture. In this artistic allegory, Rodin seeks to capture the desired image as it emerges from what appears to be a partly finished, partly unfinished, work.

RODIN. *The Sculptor's Dream*. Bronze, height 26″. Kunsthalle, Bremen

Antoine Bourdelle worked with Rodin for a time and was indebted to him for many highly important and stimulating ideas. The powerful movement in his work is also reminiscent of Rude, whose methods Bourdelle developed along new lines—those of Impressionism. As a teacher (of Alberto Giacometti and Germaine Richier), he occupies a position of considerable importance.

Attempts made in various fields of art to discover new laws of form to oppose the formlessness of Impressionism show very clearly in Adolf von Hildebrand's sculpture, particularly since his creative efforts were accompanied by exhaustive and penetrating theoretical reflections. His meeting with Hans von Marées in Rome was decisive for him and helped him to discover the classically calm form of his sculptures. His writings, particularly *The Problem of Form in the Plastic Arts* (1893) had a distinctive effect on aesthetics.

The Berlin sculptor Louis Tuaillon also belonged to that group of artists who were attracted and influenced by the great artistic talent of Hans von Marées.

ADOLF VON HILDEBRAND (1847–1921). *The Lovers*. 1909.
Wax, height 12¼″. Kunsthalle, Bremen

LOUIS TUAILLON (1862–1919). *Female Figure*. Bronze,
height 18¾″. Kunsthalle, Bremen

George Minne is one of the greatest exponents of Art Nouveau sculpture. The figure of a kneeling youth, ▶
repeated five times and mounted on the circular rim of the basin of the fountain in the Folkwang Museum
in Essen, is one of the outstanding examples of this development in art (see pages 198–99). It is a sculpture
which passes over into applied art, where it serves a utilitarian purpose, or which may conversely be said to
grow out of it. It is sculpture brought to such a degree of formality that in its ambivalent form it can combine
with the pure shape of the basin's rim and by so doing affect its character with the slightly melancholy mood
of its rhythm. Although the whole intention is to achieve purity, the total effect borders on artifice and is not
altogether free of a certain preciosity.

Constantin Meunier's art lies in an intermediate position between that of two influential contemporaries. On
one side there is Rodin, to whom he owed a great deal, although Meunier rejected his boldly uncompromis-
ing approach. On the other side is the formal purity most clearly demonstrated at that time by Hildebrand.
Then there is Meunier's unusual choice of subjects—figures of working people raised to heroic proportions,
but always containing a striving for realistic representation.

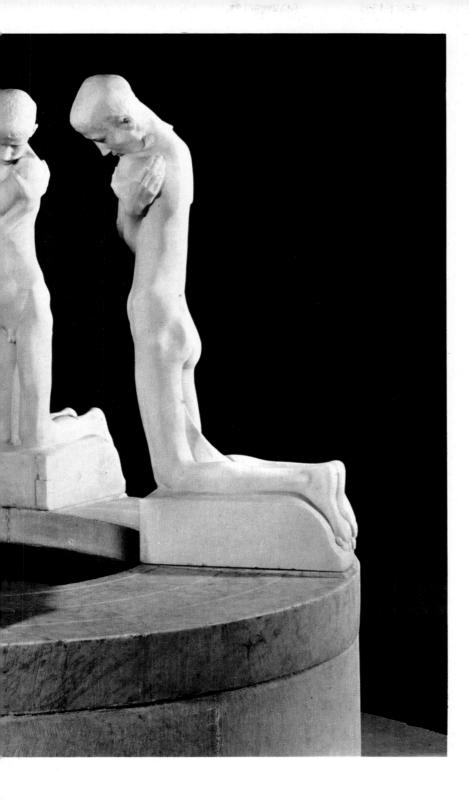

MINNE. *Fountain with Five Kneeling Youths.* 1898–1906. Marble, height of figures 30³/₄″. Folkwang Museum, Essen

MAX KLINGER (1857–1920). *Ludwig van Beethoven.* 1885–1902. Various types of marble, bronze, ivory, and molten glass, total height 10′ 2″. Museum der Bildenden Künste, Leipzig

The admiration which his contemporaries showed for Max Klinger's work was already tempered by the realization of its inherent contradictions: it was threatened by the very fact of its eclecticism. Klinger experimented in reviving the multicolored sculpture of Antiquity and, in doing so, improved on similar experiments made earlier in the century. These efforts reach their peak with the *Beethoven* statue (facing page), constructed from variously colored marbles, bronze, ivory, and colored molten glass.

ARCHITECTURE

Although only relatively few of the daring architectural designs of the French Revolution could actually be executed, they launched a new style of architecture in the nineteenth century. Étienne-Louis Boullée and Claude-Nicolas Ledoux were its leading exponents. The influence of buildings designed from a reduction to basic geometric or stereometric forms (forms which were symbolical) was to make itself felt well beyond the end of the century. Their enlightened rationalism, mathematical principles, and tendency to turn back to the primitive in a somewhat Romantic manner are in accord with the revolutionary atmosphere at the dawn of the new age, with new ideas being mixed with Baroque and Late Baroque trends. Friedrich Gilly, the pioneer of German Neoclassicism, was profoundly affected by this architecture.

CLAUDE-NICOLAS LEDOUX (1736–1806). *Design for House of the Director of the Loue River;* part of project for the saltworks of Chaux, Arc-et-Senans (Franche-Comté). c. 1775. Bibliothèque Nationale, Paris

ÉTIENNE-LOUIS BOULLÉE (1728–1799). *Design for a Funerary Chapel,* for an imaginary city. c. 1789–99. Bibliothèque Nationale, Paris

'Rulers and architects, however different their political attitudes, were all presented with the challenges of the era of the masses. In the chaos of the Revolution little could actually be achieved. The outstanding Utopian projects remained on paper; even so, they served as the starting point for the new architecture. The two most important artists were Étienne-Louis Boullée (1728–1799) and Claude-Nicolas Ledoux (1736–1806). The dictum of a speaker in the 1793 convention, 'L'architecture doit se régénérer par la géométrie,' had been their maxim for some time past. In spite of their considerable archaeological knowledge, they were not academic classicists but belong to the ranks of great Utopians essential at times to the progress of architecture'' (K. Lankheit).

Ledoux, until the outbreak of the Revolution, was a busy and popular architect whose buildings show the transition from the classical French style to Neoclassicism. It has often been pointed out how, early in his career, he rejected the architectural style of Baroque feudalism and developed instead a new type of cubical building.

ALEXANDRE BRONGNIART (1739–1813). *Design for the Bourse,* Paris. Begun 1808. Musée Carnavalet, Paris

The design for the Bourse, like the Madeleine, has a freestanding colonnade which, like that of a peripteral temple, surrounds a building of roughly square outline. H. R. Hitchcock points to the similarity between its interior and the style of Louis XIV, and describes this regression as typical of this stage of "Romantic Classicism."

The Madeleine church is representative of "State Classicism" as an architectural style in the time of Napoleon I. The Emperor saw himself as a descendant of the Roman Caesars and accordingly his ideas on building took the form of Roman monuments such as temples, columns, arches, and triumphal ways.

The Madeleine was built originally in 1809 as a *Temple de la Gloire* and was not converted into a Christian church until 1816. The range of Napoleonic buildings in Paris includes the Vendôme Column, based on Trajan's Column, the Arc du Carrousel (see page 206), and the Arc de Triomphe (page 207). This last merits special attention on account of its new stylistic approach.

JACQUES- (or JEAN-) FRANÇOIS DELANNOY (1755–1835). *Design for the Madeleine*, Paris. Musée Carnavalet, Paris

Charles Percier (1764–1838) and Pierre-François-Léo-
nard Fontaine (1762–1853). Arc du Carrousel, Paris. 1806–8

Jean-François-Thérèse Chalgrin (1739–1811) ▶
and others. Arc de Triomphe, Paris. 1806–36

The triumphal arch represents a type of building which belongs to Antiquity, when it was used as a memorial to celebrate a victory or conquest and usually to honor an emperor. The two Parisian edifices are based on Roman models, but the Arc de Triomphe surpasses all other comparable buildings. The absence of the usual columns means that the unimpeded bulk of the building is left free to impress, and its somber harmony is thrown into prominence. These are qualities that remind us of the serious aspirations of Revolutionary architecture. The Arc du Carrousel, on the other hand, is closely modeled on the Arch of Septimius Severus. These two buildings mark the beginning and end of the great axis running between the Louvre and the Place Charles de Gaulle (formerly Place de l'Étoile).

The main body of Peter Speth's work is in the tradition of French Revolutionary architecture. His use of classical motifs, divorced from their traditional setting, to produce a simpler, more concise language depending on the massive cubical appearance of the building, was to have a considerable influence on nineteenth-century architecture.

Friedrich August Stüler's Mint in Berlin, showing Renaissance leanings, replaced a building by H. Gentz, constructed in 1798–1800 in a Roman-classical style. Stüler took only the relief frieze from Gentz's building to transfer to the new mint. This relief was executed by Gottfried Schadow from a design by Friedrich Gilly, and its scenes illustrate pictorially the meaning and function of the building, i.e., the monetary system and architecture. The frieze has been in storage since the demolition of Stüler's building in 1934.

FRIEDRICH AUGUST STÜLER (1800–1865). Former Mint, Berlin. Built from his design in 1868–71; destroyed in 1934; photographed c. 1930

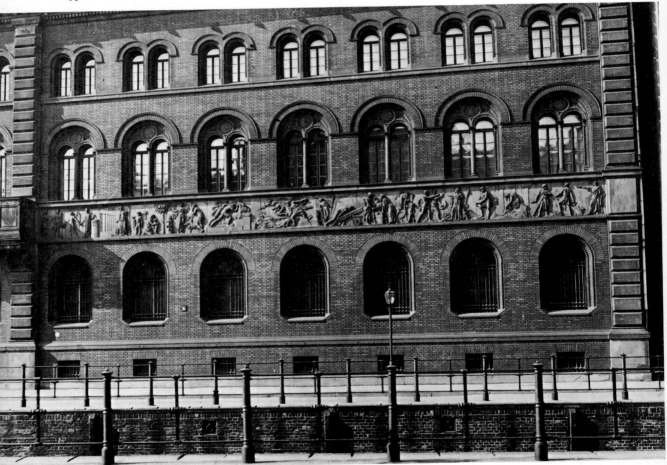

208

KARL GOTTHARD LANGHANS (1733–1808). Brandenburg Gate, Berlin. 1789

Karl Gotthard Langhans's Brandenburg Gate in Berlin is one of the most remarkable works of its time. Built in the fateful year 1789, it stands out against the great Baroque architecture and the Neoclassicism of the West, setting the standard for the nineteenth century. The architect "as he himself stated, chose as his model the Propylaea on the Acropolis, which he knew from etchings. Langhans, who until then had not been particularly prominent in his provincial Silesian environment, was inspired to this artistic achievement of unique value both by the idealistic spirit of the period and by the nature of the task, which consisted of providing a fitting introduction to the great Prussian triumphal way 'Unter den Linden.' Six Doric columns on each side, set on socles (contrary to classical rules) and held together by interconnecting walls, carry the massive attic story. The projecting central part of this serves as a base for Gottfried Schadow's powerful quadriga. The lower guardrooms, temple-shaped in design, are attached at right angles to the Gate. This Prussian adaptation of something Greek, which had also shaped Kant's, Fichte's, and Humboldt's ethos in a similar way, ushered in a new style of thinking in architecture. This found expression in its most basic and purest form in the work of Langhans's student, who died while still young" (K. Lankheit). The student was Friedrich Gilly, whose design for the monument to Frederick the Great was not only the most daring plan for a memorial in Germany's architectural history but also shaped German Neoclassicism and initiated its further development. "He intended that in the center of the octagonally shaped Leipziger Platz a Doric peripteral temple of a light-colored material with bronze pediment reliefs should rise above a darker-colored substructure consisting of great cubelike masses, vaulted entrances, and arrangements of Doric columns. In the cella of the temple, the deceased was to be enthroned like Jupiter. A massive gateway flanked by colonnaded halls, paired obelisks, and water-spouting lions enlarged the whole design to create a sacred thoroughfare. Both the daring of the plan and the overpowering effect of the sculptural masses of the building make this a design unique in Germany" (K. Lankheit). At the same time, Gilly's style is reminiscent of French Revolutionary architecture. He came to be the leading architect of German Neoclassicism and was, moreover, the founder of modern theater design. His drawings of Marienburg Castle opened the eyes of his contemporaries to medieval architecture. Karl Friedrich Schinkel, Gilly's student, developed his teacher's ideas in a pioneering spirit, and in doing so carried forward certain fundamental proportions present in Langhans's Brandenburg Gate.

FRIEDRICH GILLY (1771–1800). *Design for Monument to Frederick the Great*. 1796. Technische Universität, Berlin

"England, since the days of Inigo Jones, was in possession of an unbroken classical tradition. Early in the eighteenth century, Wren's Baroque classicism was replaced by Lord Burlington's Palladianism, a style internationally important as being diametrically opposed to Late Baroque and Rococo. In 1762, James Stuart and Nicholas Revett published the first volume of their epoch-making *Antiquities of Athens*. The Adam brothers, Scotsmen like Stuart, created in the 1770s a particular classicizing style parallel to the Louis XVI and *Zopf-stil* [Late Rococo] of the Continent. In 1790, this Adam style had to give way to Romantic Neoclassicism. It was, admittedly, a highly personally colored expression of the general style of the era" (K. Lankheit).

JOHN SOANE (1753–1837) architect; JOSEPH MICHAEL GANDY (1771–1843) draftsman. *Group of Churches to Illustrate Different Styles of Architecture*. c. 1825. Watercolor, 29$\frac{1}{2}$ × 51$\frac{1}{2}$". Sir John Soane's Museum, London

John Nash and Sir John Soane were England's leading architects in the first half of the nineteenth century. Soane, after studying at the London Academy, was considerably influenced by his stay in Rome, where he was still able to meet Piranesi. His classicism is undogmatic and elegant. A general striving after simplified forms unites him with his French and German contemporaries, although his buildings are free from the dramatic starkness that, coming particularly from French sources, affected the general architecture of the period.

SOANE; draftsman unknown. *Design for the Rotunda of the Bank of England.* 1798. Watercolor, 24³/₄ × 27¹/₂″. Sir John Soane's Museum, London

J. M. Gandy, a painter and architect and student of James Wyatt, was chiefly employed, from 1811 on, by Soane as a draftsman. In spite of his own enormous talent, he did not succeed in obtaining important commissions. It is sometimes thought that Soane's later designs are based in part on Gandy's ideas. The picture reproduced on the opposite page points out a characteristic of nineteenth-century architecture—that is, the option of being able to choose from a number of alternative designs.

Christian Frederik Hansen is one of the great masters of Danish–North German Neoclassicism. His design for the Vor Frue Kirke in Copenhagen takes into account the foundations of the hall church that was destroyed by fire in 1807, and in the place of which he built a barrel-vaulted nave closed by a rounded apse. In this way, he reduced the importance of the aisles and transformed them into simple covered passages. Coolness and strength expressed in the Antique detailing of its forms characterize the interior space that is so reminiscent of Roman architecture. From the outset, Hansen regarded the decorative statues as an integral part of his design.

CHRISTIAN FREDERIK HANSEN (1756–1845). *Design for Vor Frue Kirke*, Copenhagen. 1811–29

GOTTLIEB BINDESBØLL (1800–1856). Thorvaldsen Museum, Copenhagen. 1839–48

Gottlieb Bindesbøll knew Bertel Thorvaldsen as a friend, and developed the designs for Thorvaldsen's museum while staying in Rome, where the great sculptor, too, was living. The plans followed the lines of an old coaching house that had stood on the site. Here, Bindesbøll created a two-storied building with painted facades: on the outside, there are representations of Thorvaldsen's life, and inside, palms, oaks, laurels, and genii surround the sculptor's tomb in the center of the court.

As a continuation of Friedrich Gilly's interest in medieval architecture and as precursor of the architectural problems of the future, Karl Friedrich Schinkel, in various of his projects, heralds the revival of a monumental Gothic style. This was to attain its highest point with the completion of Cologne Cathedral, an experiment in an architectural encounter with the Middle Ages. Schinkel's executed designs are, however, mainly classicistic. His Altes Museum in Berlin is especially important as an outstanding and exemplary solution of an architectural problem that was of first importance to nineteenth-century architecture.

KARL FRIEDRICH SCHINKEL (1781–1841). Altes Museum, Berlin. 1824–28

SCHINKEL. *Stage Design for the Opera* Ondine: *The Marketplace.* 1816. Gouache, $13^3/_4 \times 19^3/_4''$. Kupferstichkabinett und Sammlung der Zeichnungen, Staatliche Museen, Berlin. Schinkel Collection

The Altes Museum is a rectangular building fronted by a portico supported by eighteen Ionic columns as its main facade. A flat, square structure in the very center of the museum surmounts a long colonnaded hall, and within this there is a rotunda reminiscent of the Pantheon in Rome.

SCHINKEL. School of Architecture, Berlin. 1832–35

The functionalism of Karl Friedrich Schinkel's building is more apparent in his Berlin School of Architecture, a square edifice built round a small, rectangular inner court. The units of measurement of the ground plan are squares of 5.55 meters (18′ 2¹/₂″), a measurement that determines the vaulting of the interior as well as the organization of the facade. The facade consists of an arrangement of piers whose structure is dependent on engineering techniques: the piers were erected first and connected to each other solely by means of iron ribs; then the intermediate walls were filled in. Technology and aesthetics control each other and the possibilities of skeletal building are demonstrated.

Some ten years before Schinkel built his School of Architecture, Thomas Telford, a civil engineer who was Britain's foremost constructor of means of communication of the time, erected St. Katharine's Docks in London. His chief works include canals, aqueducts, and especially bridges. In contrast to the unobtrusive and delicate details of Schinkel's well-proportioned and elaborate buildings, Thomas Telford uses a rocklike bulkiness which, with its massive columns and the play of projecting and contrasting volumes, has a distinctive character of its own.

To begin with, Schinkel was mainly active as a painter, which is how he came to be employed as a theatrical designer, a trade he learned from Wilhelm Gropius. He preferred architectural scenery on only few planes, parallel to the footlights, concentrated, and with a classical clarity that accorded well with his use of a cool coloring.

SCHINKEL. *Stage Design for* The Magic Flute: *Sarastro's Temple.* 1815. Gouache, $20\frac{1}{4} \times 24\frac{1}{2}''$. Kupferstichkabinett und Sammlung der Zeichnungen, Staatliche Museen, Berlin. Schinkel Collection

SCHINKEL. *Stage Design for* The Magic Flute: *Appearance of the Queen of the Night.* 1815. Gouache, 18^1/$_4$ × 24^1/$_8$". Kupferstichkabinett und Sammlung der Zeichnungen, Staatliche Museen, Berlin. Schinkel Collection

Among Schinkel's numerous activities, which embraced all the architectural tasks of his period, including the industrial arts, the care of ancient monuments, and town planning, those of his designs that were never carried out deserve just as much consideration for their influence on the history of art and philosophy of the nineteenth century. This applies especially to his designs for a royal palace in Athens (see page 222).

SCHINKEL. *Design for the Throneroom of a Royal Palace on the Acropolis of Athens.* 1834. Watercolor and distemper, 22^1/$_4$ × 16^3/$_4$". ▶ Kupferstichkabinett und Sammlung der Zeichnungen, Staatliche Museen, Berlin. Schinkel Collection

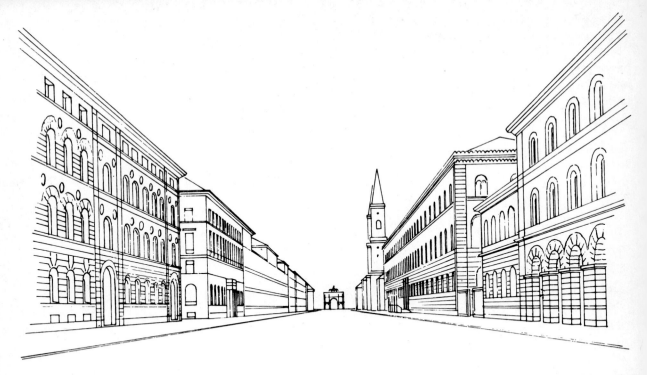

KLENZE and FRIEDRICH VON GÄRTNER (1792–1847). Ludwigstrasse, Munich, looking north toward the Siegestor. Begun 1817

◄ LEO VON KLENZE (1784–1864). Valhalla, near Regensburg. 1830–42

The interior (a memorial hall with Ionic features, housing busts of the elect) of Leo von Klenze's Valhalla (see page 223)—a building representative of an idealistic longing for Greece—is reminiscent of Schinkel's visions, though in a conflicting sense. The roof of this classicizing building is carried on iron rafters.

Valhalla, together with the Siegesallee in Berlin, the Panthéon in Paris, and the sculptures on Monte Pincio in Rome, represents a certain nineteenth-century attitude toward memorials which springs from a desire to put on display whole sequences of ancestors and traditions.

Leo von Klenze's architecture had a considerable effect on the character of Munich, where he erected thirty buildings for Ludwig I. His designs for the Ludwigstrasse (facing page) draw on Italian Renaissance influences. Here, he created a type of thoroughfare by enclosing an elongated open square at the upper end by a ceremonial gate, and at the lower by a loggia. The street stretching between the Royal Palace (Residenz) and the University, was to contain a church and other important buildings. At Ludwig I's own wish, Klenze modeled the facade of the palace on that of the Palazzo Pitti in Florence.

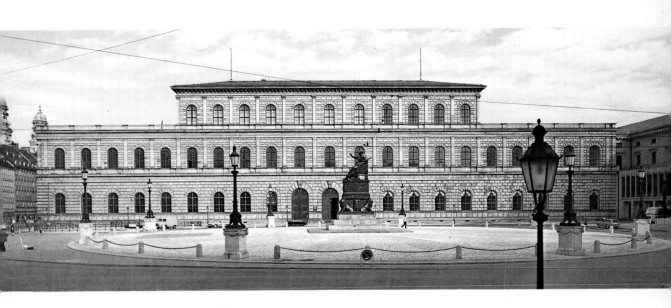

KLENZE. Royal Palace, Munich. 1825

GOTTFRIED SEMPER (1803–1879). Neues Hoftheater (Opera House), Dresden. 1871–78
Built to replace the previous theater, also built by Semper and destroyed by fire in 1868

"The young artist hurries through the world, stuffs his herbarium with well-mounted tracings of every kind, and returns home, full of good cheer in the happy anticipation that a commission for a Valhalla à la Parthenon, a basilica à la Monreale, a boudoir à la Pompeii, a palace à la Pitti, a Byzantine church, or even a bazaar in the Turkish style will not be long in coming," wrote Gottfried Semper in 1834. Semper rebelled against the confusing mixture of styles in his times and went on to say that "our era, judged by its culture and aspirations, is merely a continuation of the Renaissance. Therefore, the modern architect has a duty above all to reconsider the actuality of the Renaissance and to develop it further."

Semper became influential also because of his theoretical dissertations—about the polychromatic style of Greek architecture and sculpture, the Italian Renaissance as arbiter between Antique and modern architecture, and generally about style and technique. His Dresden buildings are masterpieces. The Art Gallery shuts off the unfinished court of the Zwinger on the Elbe side and attempts, through a more elaborate, sculptural construction, to approximate to the Rococo. Only later, with his posthumously executed buildings in Vienna, did Semper become the forerunner of a Neo-Baroque development.

The Dresden theater (facing page), mainly because of the clarity with which it solved the problem of outline, is considered to be a landmark in theater design.

SEMPER. Neues Museum (Art Gallery), Dresden. 1847–54

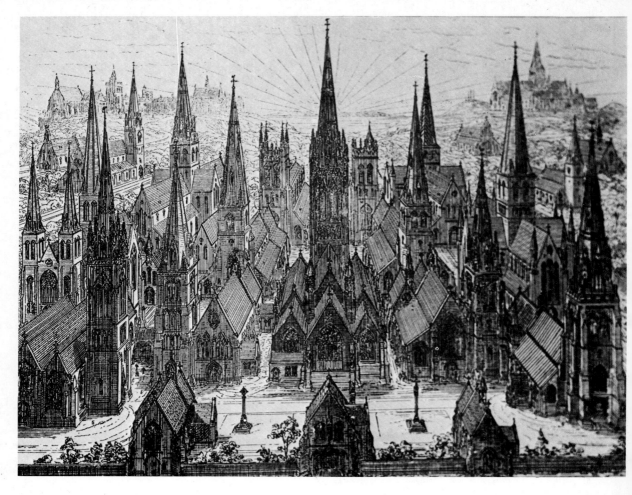

AUGUSTUS WELBY NORTHMORE PUGIN (1812–1852).
The Present Revival of Christian Architecture.
Frontispiece to *An Apology for the Revival.* 1843

Cologne Cathedral: The Porch, as it was intended to be.
Steel engraving from drawing by G. Molley. 1813. 29 ×
19³/₄″. Graphische Sammlung, Stadtmuseum, Cologne

The illustration above shows a number of church designs by Pugin. His admiration for things medieval, especially Gothic, came to be a moving force of his work. This prospect takes on new meaning as a representation of a dreamlike vision of a medieval town.

The building of Cologne Cathedral was started in 1248, but was left unfinished in the Middle Ages; no work was done on it after 1560. In 1814, Joseph von Görres, writing in the *Rheinischer Merkur,* called for its completion. In this he followed a considerable tradition, similar demands having been made ever since the seventeenth century. The enormous task of completing the building would not have been possible before the nineteenth century, when it became the crowning achievement of the century's Gothic revival, becoming a matter of concern for the German nation as well as arousing international interest. In 1804, the Empress Josephine donated money for minor restoration work. In 1840 Friedrich Wilhelm IV sanctioned the continuation of

ERNST FRIEDRICH ZWIRNER (1802–1861). Apollinaris Church, Remagen. 1839–43. Graphische Sammlung, Stadtmuseum, Cologne

building. From 1808 on, Sulpiz Boisserée was drawing up plans in his survey, and in 1814 and 1816, some of the original designs were rediscovered. Schinkel's survey and estimates played their part in the continuation of the building. The work was begun in 1833 with Ernst Friedrich Zwirner as chief architect, followed by Richard Voigtel in 1862. The monumental edifice has a self-confidence shown generally in this era in the face of all doubts and difficulties. It is sometimes said that we, nowadays, have lost this naive ability to defy history, with its devastation and its obstacles. But the rebuilding of the cities of Europe after the Second World War poses this question anew.

The "Society of Cathedral Builders" of Ernst Friedrich Zwirner, Schinkel's pupil, set an example for all European architects concerned with the restoration of old buildings. Zwirner's greatest work is the Apollinaris Church in Remagen, a Neo-Gothic building that exhibits Neoclassical traits and is reminiscent of Schinkel's interpretation of this style of architecture. As part of the renewed interest in the much admired examples provided by the Middle Ages, an attack was made in 1820 on a long-standing problem, namely the never completed facade of Florence Cathedral, for which various solutions were sought. The final form ties in with the campanile, giving its elements a new unity and a stronger sculptural effect.

EMILIO DE FABRIS (1808–1883). Facade of the Cathedral, Florence. 1875–87

HEINRICH VON FERSTEL (1828–1883). Votivkirche. Vienna. 1856–79

JEAN-BAPTISTE-ANTOINE LASSUS (1807–1857). Church of St.-Jean-Baptiste-de-Belleville, Paris. 1854–59

Jean-Baptiste-Antoine Lassus, antagonistic to Neoclassicism, became the protagonist of a radical Neo-Gothic style. The building shown above demonstrates a new variation of the Early Gothic French cathedral style.

Ferstel's Votivkirche in Vienna (facing page), a freer adaptation of the fourteenth-century style, is considered one of the most important Neo-Gothic buildings. Its elegant, brittle form differs strikingly from the Early Gothic variants of Lassus.

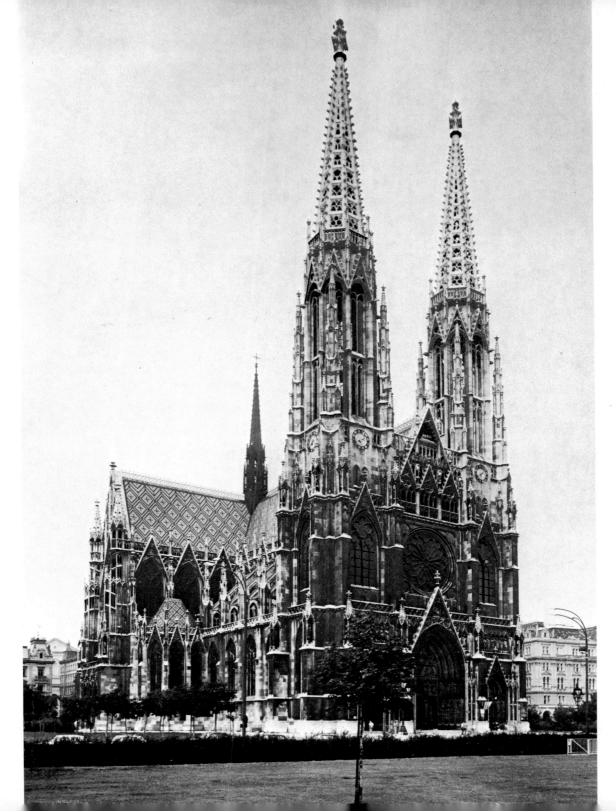

The greatest commission in France in the nineteenth century, the Paris Opéra, went to Charles Garnier, an architect previously quite unknown. He obtained the commission in 1860 as the result of a public competition. His "Napoleon III style" brought about a revival of interest in the Baroque and introduced the Neo-Baroque into France. The plan of the Opéra accords with a widespread style of theater building introduced by Victor Louis with the Bordeaux theater. The great open staircase, which in Garnier's design leads up within the building to the various higher levels, attracted particular attention.

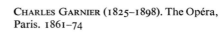

EDUARD RIEDEL (1813–1885). Schloss Neuschwanstein, Bavaria. Begun 1868, based on ideas provided by Ludwig II and his theatrical designer Christian Jank

Ludwig II of Bavaria took an active part in designing his castles, which are veritable masterpieces of historicist architecture.

Herrenchiemsee (facing page) closely resembles Versailles, the palace of Louis XIV, whose brilliant world appealed to the eccentric Bavarian king. He was particularly influenced by the bedchamber and the Hall of Mirrors of the French palace.

GEORG VON DOLLMANN (1830–1895). Hall of Mirrors, Schloss Herrenchiemsee, Bavaria. Begun 1878 ▶

DOLLMANN and JULIUS HOFMANN (1840–1896).
Schloss Linderhof, Bavaria. Begun 1870

If Herrenchiemsee was Ludwig II's Versailles, then Neuschwanstein (page 236) was his Wartburg. The interior is decorated with representations of motifs from Richard Wagner's operas. Ludwig was fascinated by Wagner's artistic personality and his operatic themes led the king to design a further medieval castle. Ludwig's architectural ideas had their beginning not only in Wagner's work but more generally in the world of the theater: he would frequently commission appropriate plays to be written and performed in order to stimulate new designs. Schloss Linderhof is the most intimate and pleasant creation of this kind, which, despite all its borrowings from Baroque and Rococo, does not look back to any particular model for its inspiration.

Biedermeier is a middle-class style which brought forth its own characteristic range in furniture design. Occasionally it adopts Empire forms, although on the whole it repudiates this development (of about 1800–30) with furniture that no longer yearns after artistic grandeur. Instead, its neater, pleasing shapes are simple and purposeful. Plain cubes are combined with segments of circles and ovals and their stereometric counterparts; together with the light, warm texture of the wood, they produce an impression of homeliness. Their bourgeois character is imprinted even on pieces like the one illustrated on this page, which comes from the collection of the Archduchess Sophie at Schloss Laxenburg, near Vienna.

Sewing table in the form of a globe

The new nineteenth-century building methods are not always hidden behind ornamental facings. Interest centered especially on the technical problems and led to new styles in design. Eugène-Emmanuel Viollet-le-Duc praised the extraordinary adaptability of this type of construction and suggested that the iron components could be manufactured on an industrial scale (see page 242).

In the hall of the Oxford University Museum (page 243), the iron-skeleton construction supporting the glass roof, with its Neo-Gothic flavor, stands quite independently. Some of its members have painted ornamentation and are decorated with wrought-iron plant forms. The iron roof construction over the central space is surrounded by walls closely modeled on Venetian architecture.

EUGÈNE-EMMANUEL VIOLLET-LE-DUC (1814–1879). *Joining of Iron Frame* ▶
and Brick Vaulting. 1865. From his *Entretiens sur l'architecture, 1858–72*

The mixture of styles of this cabinet (Baroque and Renaissance) reflects Semper's interest in the styles of past ages, but at the same time contradicts his condemnation of stylistic pluralism.

◄ Thomas Deane (1792–1871) and Benjamin Woodward (1815–1861). University Museum, Oxford. 1855–60

Edward William Godwin's designs were intended for industrial manufacture. His clearly constructed forms are developed from English Neo-Gothic, refined by a study of Japanese crafts.

EDWARD WILLIAM GODWIN (1833–1886). Sideboard. c. 1877. Victoria & Albert Museum, London

August Endell's Atelier Elvira is one of the finest examples of Art Nouveau architecture, which appears in many different forms but which here demonstrates some of its basic principles. The character of the whole building is determined by the ornamentation which, set flat on the facade, strives to whirl away the other static shapes by its own motion. This is not a case of decorative forms growing out of the structural character of an architectural concept; on the contrary, here it is the ornament that determines the architecture, e.g., the outlines and internal framework of windows and door. It is the generous and striking execution of this principle that makes Endell's building memorable; its relatively conventional outline is otherwise insignificant. Other examples of European architecture of this period show how Art Nouveau could affect the whole outline of the building.

AUGUST ENDELL (1871–1925). Atelier Elvira, Munich. 1897–98. Destroyed in 1944

ANTONI GAUDÍ (1852–1926). Steps in Park Güell, Barcelona. Begun 1900

Antoni Gaudí's art, as seen in the buildings of Park Güell and the still incomplete Church of the Sagrada Familia in Barcelona, is in the historicist tradition and yet has passed beyond it. The tradition is replaced by an overflowing imagination, freely creating shapes, partly vegetable, partly abstract in form. In this way, a new architecture develops which disregards the traditional functions of load and load bearing by optical means and resolves them in complex formulas. In some ways, especially in the rejection of traditional forms and the free interplay of fluid architectural elements, this work makes common cause with Art Nouveau. At the same time, Gaudí's fantastic configurations are reminiscent of Baroque and Mannerist developments. Simultaneously, they appear as a typical statement of Spanish art, which occupies a special place among European traditions.

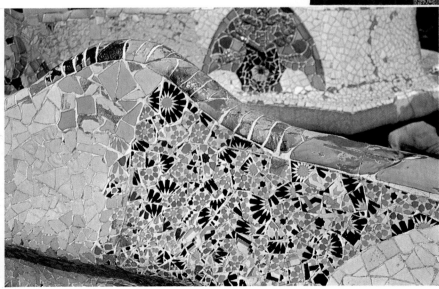

GAUDÍ. Detail of curving parapet of terrace, Park Güell, Barcelona. 1911

Since the eighteenth century, the problems of bridge building had been tackled with new understanding, especially by J.-R. Perronet, whose constructions were more firmly based on whole series of tests and calculations. The development of steel bridges followed the progress made in iron and steel production. The first cast-iron bridge was built in England at Coalbrookdale, Shropshire (in 1777–79), and on the European mainland at Laasan in Silesia (1794–96). The Britannia Bridge over the Menai Strait was the first bridge to be built of welded iron girders. The first metal frame bridge was built in England in 1851.

It is bridge building that shows most plainly the new solutions arising from the combination of visual effects and technical problems in approaching a common task. Robert Stephenson solves it by constructing a new kind of tubular bridge, square in cross-section, self-supporting, and without chain suspension. It rests on only three piers and spans a length of approximately five hundred yards. The masonry abutments erected by Francis Thompson, with their huge lion sculptures, conform to the functional construction of the bridge.

ROBERT STEPHENSON (1803–1859) and FRANCIS THOMPSON. Britannia Bridge, Menai Strait, Wales. 1846–50

FRANZ ANDREAS MEYER (1837–1901) and others.
Bridge over the Norderelbe, Hamburg. 1884–88

The bridge in Hamburg shows the contrast, frequently found in this period, between a building style imposed by the static function of metal construction and stone portals derived from North German Gothic brickwork. The portals were demolished in the course of later rebuilding.

ALEXANDRE-GUSTAVE EIFFEL (1832–1923). Eiffel Tower, Paris.
Erected 1887–89 for the World Exhibition of 1889. Height 984′

The Eiffel Tower in Paris was hailed in its day, and especially by the artists of the time, as a symbol of a new epoch: Guillaume Apollinaire praised it in his poems; it appears in Robert Delaunay's paintings. Its elegant form grew directly out of developments in the technical possibilities of iron construction. Its use as a viewing tower is only secondary—it is in its role as a unique monument to an architectural style that the Eiffel Tower's importance lies.

Bibliography

GENERAL WORKS

ANTAL, F., "Reflections in Classicism and Romanticism" in *Burlington Magazine*, LXVI, 1935, pp. 159–68; LXVIII, 1936, pp. 130–39; LXXVII, 1940, pp. 72–80; LXXVIII, 1941, pp. 14–22

BAUCH, K., "Klassik–Klassizistik–Klassizismus" in *Das Werk des Künstlers*, I, 1939/40, pp. 429–40

HALLBAUM, F., *Der Landschaftsgarten: Sein Entstehen und seine Einführung in Deutschland durch Friedrich Ludwig von Skell, 1750–1823*, Munich, 1927

HAMANN, R., *Der Impressionismus in Leben und Kunst*, Marburg a. d. Lahn, 1923

HAMANN, R., and HERMAND, J., *Deutsche Kunst und Kultur von der Gründerzeit bis zum Expressionismus*, I: *Gründerzeit*, Berlin, 1965

HAUSER, A., *The Social History of Art*, New York, 1951, 2 vols.

HILDEBRANDT, H., *Die Kunst des 19. und 20. Jahrhunderts*, Wildpark-Potsdam, 1924

"Historismus und bildende Kunst: Vorträge und Diskussionen im Oktober 1963," *Studien zur Kunst des 19. Jahrhunderts*, I, Munich, 1965

HOFMANN, W., *The Earthly Paradise: Art in the 19th Century*, New York, 1961

HOLT, E. G., *Documentary Sources of Art*, III: *From the Classicists to the Impressionists*, New York, 1966

"Kunstgeschichte und Kunsttheorie im 19. Jahrhundert," *Probleme der Kunstwissenschaft*, I, Berlin, 1963

LANKHEIT, K., *Revolution und Restauration*, Baden-Baden, 1965

LAVIGNINO, E., *L'arte moderna dai neoclassici ai contemporanei*, Turin, 1961, 2 vols.

LIETZMANN, H., "Bibliographie zur Kunstgeschichte des 19. Jahrhunderts: Publikationen der Jahre 1940–1966," *Studien zur Kunstgeschichte des 19. Jahrhunderts*, IV, Munich, 1968

LORCK, C. VON, *Die Klassik und der Osten Europas vom Ursprung und Wesen des Klassizismus*, Oldenburg and Hamburg, 1966

MEIER-GRAEFE, J., *Entwicklungsgeschichte der modernen Kunst*, Munich, 1966, 2 vols.

NOVOTNY, F., *Painting and Sculpture in Europe, 1780–1880*, Baltimore, 1960

PAULI, G., *Die Kunst des Klassizismus und der Romantik*, Berlin, 1925

PEVSNER, N., *Academies of Art: Past and Present*, Cambridge, Mass., 1940

PEVSNER, N., *Pioneers of Modern Design: From William Morris to Walter Gropius*, New York, 1964

PONENTE, N., *Structures of the Modern World, 1850–1900*, Cleveland, 1965

"Problems of the 19th and 20th Centuries," *Studies in Western Art: Acts of the 20th International Congress of the History of Art*, edited by M. Meiss, IV, Princeton, N.J. 1963

The Romantic Movement (cat.), London, 1959

SCHEFFLER, K., *Die europäische Kunst im 19. Jahrhundert*, Berlin, n.d.–1927, 2 vols.

SCHEYER, E., *Biedermeier in der Literatur- und Kunstgeschichte*, Würzburg, 1960

SEDLMAYR, H., *Verlust der Mitte: Die bildende Kunst des 19. und 20. Jahrhunderts als Symbol der Zeit*, Salzburg, 1948

WALDMANN, E., *Die Kunst des Realismus und des Impressionismus im 19. Jahrhundert*, Berlin, 1927

PAINTING AND DRAWING

GENERAL WORKS

BRION, M., *Art of the Romantic Era*, New York and London, 1966

COLLIN, P., *La Peinture européene au XIX siècle*, Brussels and Paris, 1935

FOCILLON, H., *La Peinture aux XIX et XX siècles du réalisme à nos jours*, Paris, 1928

HEISE, C. G., *Grosse Zeichner des 19. Jahrhunderts*, Berlin, 1960

BELGIUM AND THE NETHERLANDS

COLLIN, P., *La Peinture belge depuis 1830*, Brussels, 1930

HUEBNER, F. M., *Die Kunst der niederländischen Romantik*, Düsseldorf, 1942

HYMANS, H. S., *Belgische Kunst des 19. Jahrhunderts*, Leipzig, 1906

KNOEF, J., *Tussen Rococo en Romantiek*, The Hague, 1943

KNOEF, J., *Van Romantiek tot Realisme*, The Hague, 1947

LEMONNIER, C., *L'École belge de peinture, 1830–1905*, Brussels, 1906

ROOSES, M., *Dutch Painters of the 19th Century*, London, 1898–1901, 4 vols.

ENGLAND

FREDEMAN, W. E., *Pre-Raphaelitism: A Bibliocritical Study*, Cambridge, Mass., 1965

HARTLAUB, G. F., *Die grossen englischen Maler der Blütezeit, 1750–1840*, Munich, 1948

MEIER-GRAEFE, J., *Die grossen Engländer*, Munich, 1908

REYNOLDS, G., *Victorian Painting*, New York, 1966

RITCHIE, A. C., *Masters of British Painting, 1800–1950* (cat.), Museum of Modern Art, New York, 1956

WALDMANN, E., *Englische Malerei*, Berlin, 1927

FRANCE

BERGER, K., *French Master Drawings of the 19th Century*, New York, 1950

BÜRGER-THORÉ, W., *Französische Kunst im 19. Jahrhundert*, Leipzig, 1911, 3 vols.

CHASSÉ, C., *Le Mouvement symboliste dans l'art du XIXᵉ siècle*, Paris, 1947

CHATELET, A., THUILLIER, J., and LEYMARIE, J., *French Painting, III: Nineteenth Century from David to Seurat*, Cleveland, 1962

FORGES, M. T. DE, *Barbizon*, Paris, 1962

FRANCASTEL, P., *Histoire de la peinture française, la peinture de chevalet du XIXe au XXe siècle*, II: *Du classicism au cubisme*, Paris and New York, 1955

FRIEDLÄNDER, W. F., *David to Delacroix*, Cambridge, Mass., 1952

HERBERT, R. L., *Barbizon Revisited*, New York, 1962

HUNTER, S., *Modern French Painting, 1855–1956*, New York, 1956

LEYMARIE, J., *Impressionism*, Cleveland, 1955, 2 vols.

MATHEY, F., *The Impressionists*, New York, 1961

NOCHLIN, L., *Impressionism and Post-Impressionism, 1874–1904*, Englewood Cliffs, N.J., 1966

NOCHLIN, L., *Realism and Tradition in Art, 1848–1900*, Englewood Cliffs, N.J., 1966

NOVOTNY, F., *Die grossen französischen Impressionisten: Ihre Vorläufer und ihre Nachfolge*, Vienna, 1952

RAYNAL, M., *Nineteenth Century Painting from Goya to Gauguin*, Cleveland, 1952

REWALD, J., *History of Impressionism*, New York, 1961

REWALD, J., *Post-Impressionism from Van Gogh to Gauguin*, New York, 1956

WILENSKI, R. H., *Modern French Painters*, I: *1863–1903*, New York, 1940

GERMANY, AUSTRIA, AND SWITZERLAND

ANDREWS, K., *The Nazarenes: A Brotherhood of German Painters in Rome*, Oxford, 1964

DEUSCH, W., *Malerei der deutschen Romantiker und ihrer Zeitgenossen*, Berlin, 1937

GELLER, H., *Die Bildnisse der deutschen Künstler in Rom, 1800–1830*, Berlin, 1952

GELLER, H., *150 Jahre deutsche Landschaftsmalerei: Ihre Entwicklung von 1800 bis zur Gegenwart*, Erfurt, 1951

GELLER, H., *Künstler und Werk im Spiegel ihrer Zeit: Bildnisse und Bilder deutscher Maler des 19. Jahrhunderts*, Dresden, 1956

GRIMSCHITZ, B., *Die altwiener Maler, 1815–1860*, Vienna, 1961

HAMANN, R., *Die deutsche Malerei im 19. Jahrhundert*, Leipzig, 1914

HAMANN, R., *Die deutsche Malerei vom 18. bis zum Beginn des 20. Jahrhunderts*, Berlin and Leipzig, 1925

HUGGLER, M., and CETTO, A. M., *La Peinture suisse au XIXe siècle*, Basel, 1943

LANKHEIT, K., *Das Freundschaftsbild der Romantik*, Heidelberg, 1952

RAVE, P. O., *Die deutsche Malerei des 19. Jahrhunderts*, Berlin, 1949

ITALY

CECCHI, E., *Pittura italiana dell'ottocento*, Milan, 1946

GIARDELLI, M., *I macchialuoli e l'epoca loro*, Milan, 1958

VENTURI, L., and SKIRA-VENTURI, R., *Italian Painting*, III: *From Caravaggio to Modigliani*, Cleveland, 1952

RUSSIA

FIALA, V., *Die russische realistische Malerei des 19. Jahrhunderts*, Prague, 1953

GRAY, C., *The Great Experiment: Russian Art, 1863–1922*, London, 1962

LUKOMSKII, G. K., *History of Modern Russian Painting: Russian Painting of the Past Hundred Years, 1840–1940*, London, 1945

SCANDINAVIA

AUBERT, A., *Die nordische Landschaftsmalerei und Johann Christian Dahl*, Berlin, 1947

DURHAM, A., *Painting in Norway*, Stockholm, 1955

HINTZE, C., *Kopenhagen und die deutsche Malerei um 1800*, Würzburg, 1937

POULSEN, V., *Danish Painting and Sculpture*, Copenhagen, 1955

POULSEN, V., *Peinture au Danemark*, Copenhagen, 1960

UNITED STATES

BAUR, J., RÖTHEL, H. H., and SCHÄDLER, A., *Hundert Jahre Amerikanische Malerei, 1800–1900* (cat.), Munich, 1953

FLEXNER, J. T., *Light of Distant Skies*, New York, 1968

GREEN, S. M., *American Art: A Historical Survey*, New York, 1966

HUEBNER, F. U., and DELGADO, V. P., *Die Maler der Romantik in Amerika*, Bonn, 1953

LARKIN, O., *Art and Life in America*, New York, 1949

LARKIN, O., *Samuel F. B. Morse and American Democratic Art*, New York, 1954

MUMFORD, L., *The Brown Decades: A Study of the Arts in America, 1865–1895*, New York, 1955

GRAPHICS

Bild vom Stein: Die Entwicklung der Lithographie von Senefelder bis heute (cat.), Munich, 1961

GLASER, C., *Die Graphik der Neuzeit vom Anfang des 19. Jahrhunderts bis zur Gegenwart*, Berlin, 1922

RÜMANN, A., *Das illustrierte Buch des 19. Jahrhunderts in England, Frankreich und Deutschland, 1790–1860*, Leipzig, 1929

WEBER, W., *Saxa Loquuntur—Steine reden, Geschichte der Lithographie*, I: *Von den Anfängen bis 1900*, Heidelberg, 1961

DECORATIVE ARTS

KOHLHAUSEN, H., *Geschichte des deutschen Kunsthandwerks*, Munich, 1955

LEHNERT, G., *Illustrierte Geschichte des Kunstgewerbes*, II: *Das Kunstgewerbe in Barock, Rokoko, Louis XVI, Empire und neuester Zeit*, Berlin, 1907–9

ROSNER, K., *Die dekorative Kunst im 19. Jahrhundert*, Berlin, 1898

SCULPTURE

HEILMEYER, A., *Die Plastik seit Beginn des 19. Jahrhunderts*, Leipzig, 1907

LICHT, F. S., *Sculpture: The Nineteenth and Twentieth Centuries*, Greenwich, Conn., 1967

NOVOTNY, F., *Painting and Sculpture in Europe, 1780–1880*, Baltimore, 1960

OSTEN, G. VON DER, *Die deutsche Plastik des 19. Jahrhunderts in Deutschland, Österreich und der Schweiz*, Königstein i. T., 1961

ARCHITECTURE

GENERAL WORKS

BAUER, R. H., "Architektur als Kunst: Von der Grösse der idealistischen Architektur-Ästhetik und ihrem Verfall" in *Probleme der Kunstwissenschaft*, I: *Kunstgeschichte und Kunsttheorie im 19. Jahrhundert*, Berlin, 1963, pp. 133–71

BENEVOLO, L., *Storia dell'architettura moderna*, Bari, 1960

COLLINS, P., *Changing Ideals in Modern Architecture, 1750–1950*, London, 1965

GIEDION, S., *Space, Time and Architecture*, Cambridge, Mass., 1967

GRISEBACH, A., *Die Baukunst im 19. und 20. Jahrhundert*, Berlin and Neubabelsberg, 1915

HITCHCOCK, H.-R., *Architecture: Nineteenth and Twentieth Centuries*, Baltimore, 1963

HITCHCOCK, H.-R., *Modern Architecture: Romanticism and Reintegration*, New York, 1929

KAMPHAUSEN, A., *Gotik ohne Gott: Ein Beitrag zur Deutung der Neugotik und des 19. Jahrhunderts*, Tübingen, 1952

KAUFMANN, E., *Von Ledoux bis Le Corbusier: Ursprung und Entwicklung der autonomen Architektur*, Vienna and Leipzig, 1933

PEVSNER, N., *An Outline of European Architecture*, London, 1960

PEVSNER, N., *Studies in Art, Architecture and Design*, New York, 1968, 2 vols.

RICHARDS, J. M., *The Functional Tradition in Early Industrial Buildings*, London, 1958

WITTEK, K. H., *Die Entwicklung des Stahlhochbaus von den Anfängen (1800) bis zum Dreigelenkbogen (1870)*, Düsseldorf, 1964

BELGIUM AND THE NETHERLANDS

Nederland bouwt in baksteen, 1800–1940 (cat.), Rotterdam, 1941

THIENEN, F. VAN, "De bouwkunst van de laatste anderhalve eeuw" in GELDER, H. E. VAN, *Kunstgeschiedenis der Nederlanden van de middeleeuwen tot onze tijd*, II, Utrecht, 1955

ENGLAND

CASSON, H., *An Introduction to Victorian Architecture*, London, 1948

CLARK, K., *The Gothic Revival*, New York, 1962

HITCHCOCK, H.-R., *Early Victorian Architecture in Britain*, New Haven, 1954

SUMMERSON, J., *Georgian London*, Harmondsworth, 1962

TURNOR, R., *Nineteenth Century Architecture in Britain*, New York, 1950

FRANCE

BRAULT, E., *Les Architectes par leurs œuvres*, Paris, 1893, 3 vols.

LAVEDAN, P., *L'Architecture française*, Paris, 1944

GERMANY

BEENKEN, H., *Schöpferische Bauideen der deutschen Romantik*, Mainz, 1952

HARTOG, R., *Stadterweiterungen im 19. Jahrhundert*, Stuttgart, 1962

HERMANN, W., *Deutsche Baukunst des 19. und 20. Jahrhunderts*, I: *Von 1770–1840*, Breslau, 1932

ROBSON-SCOTT, W. D., *The Literary Background of the Gothic Revival in Germany: A Chapter in the History of Taste*, Oxford, 1965

SCHUMACHER, F., *Strömungen in deutscher Baukunst seit 1800*, Cologne, 1955

ITALY

MEEKS, C. V., *Italian Architecture, 1750–1914*, New Haven, 1967

PICA, A., *L'architettura moderna in Italia*, Milan, 1941

TARCHIANI, N., *L'architettura italiana dell'ottocento*, Florence, 1937

RUSSIA AND POLAND

DMOCHOWISKI, Z., *The Architecture of Poland*, London, 1956

HAMILTON, G. H., *The Art and Architecture of Russia*, Baltimore, 1954

SCANDINAVIA

FABER, T., *Dansk arkitektur*, Copenhagen, 1963

HAHR, A., *Architecture in Sweden: A Survey of Swedish Architecture Throughout the Ages and up to the Present Day*, Stockholm, 1938

UNITED STATES

CONDIT, C. W., *American Building Art*, I: *The Nineteenth Century*, New York, 1960

HAMLIN, T., *Greek Revival Architecture in America*, New York, 1944

HITCHCOCK, H.-R., *The Architecture of H. H. Richardson and His Times*, New York, 1936

	LITERATURE AND MUSIC	ARTS
1780–1790	Schiller: *The Robbers* (1781) Mozart: *The Marriage of Figaro* (1786) Mozart: *Don Giovanni* (1787) Goethe: *Iphigenie auf Tauris* (1787) Schiller: *Don Carlos* (1787) Goethe: *Egmont* (1788)	Tischbein Latour Gilly Langhans Chodowiecki
1790–1800	Mozart: *Così fan tutte* (1790) Mozart: *The Magic Flute* (1791) Goethe: *Wilhelm Meisters Lehrjahre* (1796) Schiller: *Wallenstein* (1798–99)	Guardi (died 1793) Dannecker Schadow David
1800–1810	Schiller: *Maria Stuart* (1800) Beethoven: *Fidelio* (1803–5) Kleist: *Käthchen von Heilbronn* (1810) Paganini	*Lukasbruderschaft* founded in Vienna — Nazarenes (1809) Ingres, John Crome, Runge, Canova, Prud'hon, Friedrich, Flaxman
1810–1820	First performance of *Fidelio* (final version) in Vienna (1814) First performance of Rossini's *Barber of Seville* (1816) Goethe: *Italian Journey* (1816–17) Final volume of *Fairy Tales* by Grimm brothers (1818) Schubert completes *Sixth Symphony* (1818) Schubert: *The Trout* (1819) Shelley: *Prometheus Unbound* (1820)	Nazarenes begin decoration of Casa Bartholdy in Rome (1816) Elgin Marbles bought by British government (1816) Dahl moves to Dresden Schinkel completes Neue Wache (guardhouse) (1818) and begins Schauspielhaus (theater) in Berlin (1819) Géricault completes *The Raft of the Medusa* (1819) German artists hold their first exhibition in Rome (1819)
1820–1830	First performance of Weber's *Der Freischütz* in Berlin (1821) Goethe: *Marienbader Elegie* (1823) Death of Byron (1824) First performance of Beethoven's *Ninth Symphony* (1824) Heine: *Harzreise* (1826) Eichendorff: *Memoirs of a Good-for-Nothing* (1826) Manzoni: *The Betrothed* (1827) Revival of Bach's *Matthew Passion* by Mendelssohn (1829)	Schadow: *Luther Memorial*, Wittenberg (1821) Thorvaldsen: *Christ Blessing*, Copenhagen (1821) Overbeck: *Christ's Entry into Jerusalem* (1822) Delacroix: *Massacre at Chios* (1824) Telford: Menai Strait suspension bridge (1826) Klenze: Pinakothek and Odeon, Munich (1826–36) Ingres: *Apotheosis of Homer* (1827) Delacroix: *Faust* lithographs (1828) Schinkel completes Altes Museum, Berlin (1828) Hansen: Vor Frue Kirke, Copenhagen (completed 1829)
1830–1840	Stendhal: *The Red and the Black* (1830) Chopin settles in Paris (1831) Pushkin: *Boris Godunov* (pub. 1831) Goethe: *Faust*, Part II (1832) Satirical journal *Le Charivari* founded (1832) Goethe: *Dichtung und Wahrheit* (final vol. pub. 1833) Pushkin: *Eugene Onegin* (1832/33) Mickiewicz: *Pan Tadeusz* (1834) Büchner completes *Danton's Death* (1835) First performance of Donizetti's *Lucia di Lammermoor* (1835)	Society of Nazarenes dissolved in Rome (1830) Delacroix: *Liberty Leading the People* (1830) Zwirner appointed architect to complete Cologne Cathedral (1833) Semper appointed Professor of Architecture at Dresden (1834) Ingres appointed director of French Academy in Rome (1834) Rude: *La Marseillaise* (1835–36)

	POLITICS	SCIENCE AND TECHNOLOGY
1780–1790	Start of French Revolution (1789) Constituent Assembly	Kant: *Critique of Pure Reason* (1781) Montgolfier brothers' first balloon ascent (1783) Herder: *Outlines of the Philosophy of Man* (1784–91) Meikle invents drum threshing machine (1784) Cartwright patents power loom (1785)
1790–1800	Reign of Terror of National Convention (1793–94) Napoleon's coup d'état; becomes First Consul for 10 years (1799)	Packer patents cement manufacturing process (1791) Senefelder invents lithography (c. 1796) Pestalozzi founds school at Burgdorf (1799) Schleiermacher: *Reden über die Religion* (1799)
1800–1810	Louisiana Purchase (1803) Napoleon crowned emperor (1804) Battle of Trafalgar (1805)	Fulton's steamship *Clermont* (1807) Hegel: *Phenomenology of Mind* (1807)
1810–1820	Napoleon banished to Elba (1814) Congress of Vienna (1814–15) Battle of Waterloo (1815) Germanic Confederation founded (1816) List advocates German customs union (*Zollverein*) (1819)	Stephenson's steam locomotive *Blucher* (1814) Rumohr's first publication of his Italian art studies (1818) Schopenhauer: *The World as Will and Idea* (1819) First steamship crosses the Atlantic (1819) Ampère discovers reciprocating action of electrical currents (1820)
1820–1830	Napoleon dies on St. Helena (1821) Beginning of Greek War of Independence against the Turks (1821) Declaration of Greek independence (1822) Promulgation of Monroe Doctrine (1823) Treaty of London (agreement between England, France, and Russia concerning Greek independence) (1827)	Hegel: *Philosophy of Right* (1821) Faraday discovers principles of the electric motor (1821) First passenger railroad opened in England (1825) Ohm's Law (1827) Chevreul publishes his theory of colors (1828) Baedeker's first guidebook (1829)
1830–1840	July Revolution in France (1830) Start of revolutionary movements and uprisings throughout Europe German customs union (1833) Quadruple Alliance: treaty between England, France, Spain, and Portugal to protect liberalism (1834)	Müller: *Guide to the Archaeology of Art* (1830) British Association for the Advancement of Science founded (1831) Darwin's voyage with the *Beagle* (1831–36) Clausewitz: *On War* (pub. 1833) Babbage's "analytical engine" (1833) Michelet: *Histoire de France* (1833 on) First German railroad (1835)

	LITERATURE AND MUSIC	ARTS
1830–1840	First performance of Gogol's *The Inspector General* (1836) Eckermann begins *Conversations with Goethe* (1836; completed 1848) Dickens: *Pickwick Papers* (1836–37) Dickens: *Oliver Twist* (1838) Schumann: *Scenes of Childhood* (1838) Stendhal: *The Charterhouse of Parma* (1839) Sand: *Lélia* (1839)	Klenze: Alte Pinakothek, Munich (1836) Kugler: *History of Painting* (1837) Schinkel: Collection of architectural designs (1837) Klenze: Allerheiligen-Hofkirche, Munich (1837) Steinle: Frescoes in choir of Cologne Cathedral (1838) Menzel: Illustrations for Kugler's *History of Frederick the Great* (1839)
1840–1850	*Punch* founded (1841) First performance of Adam's ballet *Giselle* (1841) Verdi: *Nabucco* (1842) Kierkegaard: *Either/Or* (1843) Dumas: *The Count of Monte Cristo* (1845) First performance of Wagner's *Tannhäuser* (1845) First performance of Hebbel's *Maria Magdalena* (1846) Thackeray: *Vanity Fair* (1848)	Rethel begins interior decoration of the Town Hall, Aachen (1840) Overbeck: *The Triumph of Religion in the Arts* (1840) Gärtner: Building started of the Feldherrnhalle, Munich (1840) Rauch: First designs for the monument to Frederick the Great in Berlin Celebrations in honor of building of Cologne Cathedral (1842) Ruskin: *Modern Painters* (begun 1843) Schwind: Frescoes started in the Kunsthalle, Karlsruhe (1843) Pugin: *An Apology for the Revival of Christian Architecture in England* (1843) Academy of Art founded in Koenigsberg (1845) Menzel: *The Balcony Room* (1845) Viollet-le-Duc starts the restoration of Notre Dame, Paris (1845) Klenze starts Propylaea in Munich (1846) Rethel: *The Dance of Death* (1849) Courbet: *Funeral at Ornans* (1849) Rietschel: Lessing Memorial, Brunswick (1849)
1850–1860	Dickens: *David Copperfield* (1850) Melville: *Moby Dick* (1851) First performance of Verdi's *Rigoletto* (1851) First performances of Verdi's *Il Trovatore* and *La Traviata* (1853) Wagner begins composition of *The Ring of the Nibelung* (1853; completed 1874) Sand: *Histoire de ma Vie* (1854) First performance of Goethe's *Faust*, Part II, in Hamburg (1854) Keller completes original version of *Green Henry* (1855) Flaubert: *Madame Bovary* (1857) Baudelaire: *The Flowers of Evil* (1857) Stifter: *Nachsommer* (1857) First performance of Offenbach's *Orpheus in the Underworld* (1858)	Menzel: *Frederick the Great at Table* (1850) Schwanthaler's *Bavaria* erected in Munich Stephenson: Britannia Bridge, Menai Strait, completed Courbet: *The Stone-Breakers* (1851) Paxton: Crystal Palace in London for the Great Exhibition Menzel appointed Director of the Berlin Academy (1853) Rude: Life-size statue of Marshall Ney Viollet-le-Duc: *Dictionnaire Raisonné de l'architecture française du XIᵉ au XVIᵉ siècle* (1854) Crystal Palace, Munich Courbet: *The Painter's Studio* (1855) Courbet establishes his "Pavillon du Réalisme" Semper appointed Professor to the Swiss Federal Polytechnic in Zurich Böcklin: *Pan in the Bullrushes* (I) (1856) Feuerbach leaves for Rome (1857) Rietschel: *Monument to Goethe and Schiller* in Weimar Carpeaux: *Neapolitan Fisherboy*

	POLITICS	SCIENCE AND TECHNOLOGY
1830–1840	Queen Victoria succeeds to British throne (1837) "Göttingen 7" protest suspension of Hanoverian constitution (1837) Chartist movement in England (1839)	Carlyle: *The French Revolution* (1837) Chevreul: *De la Loi du Contraste Simultané des Couleurs* (1839) Daguerre invents the daguerrotype (1839) Goodyear develops vulcanized rubber (1839)
1840–1850	Boers found Orange Free State in S. Africa (1842) Millennial celebrations in memory of Treaty of Verdun in Germany (1843) The Weavers' Rising in Silesia (1844) Convocation of Prussian provincial diets (1847) England: Law limiting hours of work for children and young persons to 10 hours a day (1847) February Revolution in Paris. March Revolution in Berlin and other German cities (1848) German National Assembly in Frankfurt (1848) October Revolution in Austria (1848) Risorgimento in Italy Refusal by King Friedrich Wilhelm IV of Imperial crown (1849) France restores papal supremacy in Rome against Garibaldi (1849)	List: *National System of Political Economy* (1840) Proudhon: *What is Property?* (1840) First steam pile driver in Le Creusot (1842) First systematic canalization of a city—Hamburg (1843) Feuerbach: *The Nature of Religion* (1845) Proudhon: *The Philosophy of Poverty* (1846) Marx: *The Poverty of Philosophy* (1847) Marx-Engels: *Communist Manifesto* (1848)
1850–1860	Prussia gets its constitution (1850) Louis Napoleon's coup d'état (1851) Bismarck named Prussian ambassador to Germanic Diet at Frankfurt (1851) Louis Napoleon proclaimed emperor as Napoleon III (1852) Independent state of Transvaal set up (1852) Start of Crimean War (1853) Protection of Labor law in Prussia forbids child labor Treaty of Paris ends Crimean War (1856) Declaration of Paris on maritime rights represents first codification of international law (1856) Treaty of Tientsin. China to respect embassies of the Western powers (1858) German National Union founded (1859)	Hamburg Art Collection established (1850) Krupp exhibits biggest steel crucible at the Great Exhibition, London (1851) J. and W. Grimm: *German Dictionary*, Vol. I (1852) The Hermitage opened in St. Petersburg First International Exhibition of Industry, New York (1853) Ranke: Lectures on modern history given in presence of King of Bavaria (1854) Mommsen: *History of Rome* (begun 1854) Semmering railroad opened: First line to cross the Alps Burckhardt: *The Age of Cicero* (1855) Bessemer process invented (steel) First World Exhibition in Paris Curtius: *Greek History* (1857) Carlyle: *History of Frederick the Great* (1858) Virchow publishes work on cellular pathology Darwin: *On the Origin of Species by Means of Natural Selection* (1859) Burckhardt: *The Civilization of the Renaissance in Italy* (1860)

	LITERATURE AND MUSIC	ARTS
1860–1870	First performance of Hebbel's trilogy *The Nibelungs* (1861) Turgenev: *Fathers and Sons* (1862) Hugo: *Les Misérables* (1862) Raabe: *Der Hungerpastor* (1864) First performance of Wagner's *Tristan and Isolde* (1865) Dostoyevsky: *Crime and Punishment* (1866) Dostoyevsky: *The Idiot* (1869) Tolstoy: *War and Peace* (1869)	Ingres: *The Turkish Bath* (1860) Feuerbach: *Iphigenia I* (1862) Museum of Art opened in Warsaw Paris Opéra begun (Garnier) Manet: *Le Déjeuner sur l'Herbe* (1863) Renoir: *The Painter Sisley and His Wife* (1868) Manet: *Execution of the Emperor Maximilian* (1869) Carpeaux: *Dance* erected at the Opéra, Paris The *Victory Column* started in Berlin
1870–1880	Zola begins the series of novels *Les Rougon-Macquart* (1871; completed 1893) First performance of Mussorgsky's *Boris Godunov* (1874) Grieg: Music for Ibsen's *Peer Gynt* (1874–75) First performance of Bizet's *Carmen* (1875) Opening of the Paris Opéra (1875) Tolstoy: *Anna Karenina* (1875–77) First performance of Ibsen's *Peer Gynt* (1876) Twain: *The Adventures of Tom Sawyer* (1876) First performance of Ibsen's *The Pillars of Society* (1877) Tchaikovsky: *Fourth Symphony* (1878) Ibsen: *The Doll's House* (1879) D'Annunzio: *Primo Vere* (1879) First performance of Tchaikovsky's *Eugene Onegin* (1879)	Bartholdi: First designs for the *Statue of Liberty* Semper called to Vienna (1871) Monet: *Impression—Sunrise* (1872) Böcklin: *Self-Portrait with Death Playing the Violin* Cézanne: *A Modern Olympia* (1872/3) Degas: *The Cotton-Exchange in New Orleans* (1873) Semper and Hasenauer: building of Burgtheater started in Vienna First exhibition of the Impressionists in Paris (1874) Menzel: *The Iron Mill* (1875) Renoir: *Moulin de la Galette* (1876) Monet: *Gare St-Lazare* (series) Rodin: *The Age of Bronze* (1876) Manet: *Nana* (1877) Marées: *The Three Ages of Life* (1878)
1880–1890	Dostoyevsky: *The Brothers Karamazov* (1880) First performance of Wagner's *Parsifal* (1882) First performance of Massenet's *Manon* (1884) Maupassant: *Bel-Ami* (1885) Suttner: *Lay Down Your Arms* (1889)	Exhibition of the Impressionists in Paris (1880) Gaudí begins building of the Sagrada Familia, Barcelona (1882) Seurat: *A Sunday Afternoon on the Island of La Grande Jatte* (1884) Van Gogh: *The Potato Eaters* (1885) Ensor: *The Entry of Christ into Brussels* (1888) Rodin completes *The Burghers of Calais* (1888) The Nabis Eiffel Tower (1889)
1890–1900	George: *Hymnen* (1890) First performance of Mascagni's *Cavalleria Rusticana* (1890) First performance of Leoncavallo's *Pagliacci* (1892) Debussy: *Prélude à l'Après-Midi d'un Faune* (1894) Rostand: *Cyrano de Bergerac* (1897) Ibsen: *When We Dead Awaken* (1899)	Cézanne: *The Card Players* (1890) Munch: *The Cry* (1893) Munch: *Puberty* (1894) Klinger: *Brahms Fantasy* (1894) Beardsley: *Salome* (1894) Cézanne: *The Bathers* (1895) Kollwitz: *The Weavers' Rising* (1897) Endell: Atelier Elvira, Munich (1897) Rodin: *Balzac Monument* (1897) Minne: *Fountain* (begun 1898)

	POLITICS	SCIENCE AND TECHNOLOGY
1860–1870	Lincoln becomes President of the United States (1861) American Civil War (1861–65) End of serfdom in Russia Lassalle founds the Universal German Working Men's Association in Leipzig (1863) The First International (1864) North German Confederation gets its own constitution (1867) Emperor Maximilian of Mexico executed (1867) Bebel and Liebknecht start Social Democratic Working Men's party in Eisenach (1869) Pius IX opens First Vatican Council	Reis's telephone (1861) World Exhibition in London (1862) First subway station opened in London (1863) Siemens-Martin process of steel production (1864) Haeckel: *Biogenetic Law* (1866) First transatlantic cable (1866) Marx: *Capital* (first vol. 1867) Michaux's velocipede (1867) Lesseps completes Suez Canal (1869) First transcontinental railroad in America (1869)
1870–1880	The "Ems Telegram" (1870) Franco-Prussian War (1870–71) Third Republic set up in France (1870) Bismarck made Chancellor of German Empire (1871) Cultural struggle with Roman Catholic church starts in Prussia (1872) Three Emperors' League (Germany, Austria, and Russia) (1873) Lassalle's and Marx's followers unite to form the Socialist Working Men's Party (1875) Russo-Turkish War (1877) Great Britain annexes Transvaal (1877) Anti-Socialist law passed in Germany (1878) Secret alliance between Germany and Austria (1879)	Schliemann starts excavations at Troy (1870) Dohrn founds the German Zoological Station in Naples Darwin: *The Descent of Man* (1871) Remington begins manufacture of typewriters (1873) Wundt establishes first Institute of Experimental Psychology in Leipzig (1875) Bell patents telephone (1876) Otto invents four-stroke combustion engine (1876) Edison applies for patents for his phonograph (1877) Pasteur: *Microbes* (1878) Swan's electric lamp (1878) Edison's incandescent bulb (1879) United States Geological Survey founded (1879)
1880–1890	Triple Alliance: Germany, Austria, and Italy (1882) Sickness, accident, old age, and invalidity insurance law in Germany (1883–87) Germany becomes colonial power (1884) Bismarck signs "Reinsurance Treaty" with Russia (1887) Brazil abolishes slavery, the last state to do so (1888) Internationalization of the Suez Canal (1889)	Duden: *Orthographisches Wörterbuch der Deutschen Sprache* (1880) World Exhibition in Melbourne Lesseps starts building of the Panama Canal (1881) St. Gotthard railroad opened (1882) Koch discovers tubercle bacillus (1882) Nietzsche: *Thus Spake Zarathustra* (1885) Daimler, Benz: invention of the automobile Hertz discovers electronic waves (1886)
1890–1900	Luxembourg secedes from the Netherlands (1890) August Convention between France and Russia (1891) War between Greece and Turkey (1897) First Hague Peace Conference (1899) Outbreak of Boer War (1899)	Three-color printing (1890) Nansen's expedition to the North Pole (1892) Diesel invents the diesel engine (1893) Hedin's journeys through Central Asia and Tibet (1894–98) Röntgen discovers X-Rays (1895) Marconi invents wireless telegraphy (1897) P. and M. Curie discover radium (1898) Planck's Quantum Theory (1900) Zeppelin airship (1900)

Index